THE LIFE OF A
RUSSIAN WOMAN DOCTOR

THE LIFE OF A
RUSSIAN WOMAN DOCTOR

A Siberian Memoir, 1869–1954

ANNA BEK

Translated and edited by Anne D. Rassweiler
With a foreword and additional notes by
Adele M. Lindenmeyr

INDIANA UNIVERSITY PRESS
Bloomington and Indianapolis

This book is a publication of

Indiana University Press
601 North Morton Street
Bloomington, IN 47404-3797 USA

http://iupress.indiana.edu

Telephone orders	800-842-6796
Fax orders	812-855-7931
Orders by e-mail	iuporder@indiana.edu

The paper used in this publication meets the minimum
requirements of American National Standard for
Information Sciences—Permanence of Paper for
Printed Library Materials, ANSI Z39.48-1984.

Manufactured in the United States of America

Library of Congress Cataloging-in-Publication Data

Bek, Anna Nikolaevna.
  The life of a Russian woman doctor : a Siberian
memoir, 1869–1954 / Anna Bek ; translated and edited
by Anne D. Rassweiler ; with a foreword and additional
notes by Adele M. Lindenmeyr.
       p. cm.
  Includes bibliographical references and index.
  ISBN 0-253-34460-3 (cloth : alk. paper) — ISBN 0-253-
21717-2 (pbk. : alk. paper)
  1. Bek, Anna Nikolaevna. 2. Women physicians—
Russia (Federation)—Siberia—Biography. I. Rassweiler,
Anne Dickason. II. Title.
  R534.B368A3 2004
  610'.92—dc22
                                                2004006413

1 2 3 4 5 09 08 07 06 05 04

To the Women of Siberia

CONTENTS

Illustrations

All illustrations are courtesy of Evgeny Konstantinovich Andrusevich and Albina Georgievna Shchalpegina, director of the Aksha Museum, and are reprinted here with their permission.

Foreword

The Life of a Russian Woman Doctor bears witness to my friend Anne D. Rass-weiler's exuberant love of Russian history and culture, her intrepid intellectual curiosity, and her indomitable spirit. The book originated in a research project Anne developed in the early 1990s to study how, in the wake of the 1917 Revolution's promises of female emancipation, Siberian women entered public life in the 1920s and 1930s. Traveling to Siberia in 1990, 1991, and 1993, she unearthed a number of unpublished memoirs by women from diverse social groups that seemed worthy of translation, but none matched the breadth, historical value, and charm of the autobiography written in two lined school exercise books by Dr. Anna Nikolaevna Bek. Anne decided that Anna Bek's memoirs, with their potential value to students of Russian and Soviet history, deserved a book of their own. As she narrowed the focus of the project, she traveled far and wide across a Russia that was rapidly changing after the collapse of communism in 1991: interviewing Anna Bek's daughter, other family members, and surviving acquaintances and students; mining archives in Irkutsk, Chita, and St. Petersburg; and, as the introduction describes, exploring the places where Anna Bek had lived. Despite the ravages of a cruel disease that struck her in 1997 and undermined her strength, Anne persevered in her resolve to translate and publish the memoir. By the time the illness took her life in January 2002, she had largely finished the manuscript for this book. With the consent of Anne's family, I undertook to complete the tasks necessary for final publication: checking the translation, revising some introductory material, adding explanatory notes, and completing the final editing.

As Anne immediately recognized, Anna Bek's life story is valuable for the light it sheds on several important aspects of modern Russian, Siberian, Soviet, and women's history. Born to parents with little formal education in a remote corner of eastern Siberia, Anna Bek traveled great distances both geographically and socially in her long life. Like Anne Rassweiler herself, readers of the memoir are taken on a journey across Siberia as we follow Dr. Bek's life, and gain a rare glimpse into lives lived far from the capitals of

Moscow and St. Petersburg. We see how Siberians experienced the turbulent historical events and transformations of the wars and revolutions of the early twentieth century. While textbooks tell us how educational and professional opportunities opened for women in the late nineteenth and early twentieth centuries, *The Life of a Russian Woman Doctor* reveals the roots of a girl's resolve to gain an education, the obstacles she had to overcome, and the trajectory her career might take. Her autobiography helps us to gain a deeper understanding of the humanity behind the stereotypical Russian *intelligentka,* with her faith in progress and devotion to serving society, and insight into the challenges she faced when the revolution transformed her into the "new Soviet woman." To those interested in the social history of modern science and medicine, this book illuminates the paths women trod in the early twentieth century as they began to enter scientific professions in significant numbers, and the responses to their ambitions that they encountered from parents, husbands, professors, and colleagues. Dr. Bek's account in chapter 5 of her career in Soviet universities in the 1920s and 1930s discloses the enormous impact of seemingly esoteric and academic debates on careers and lives, and the complex interplay between science and politics in the Soviet Union. Finally, students of history will find Anne's introduction interesting for the insights it gives into the pursuit of historical research, and the resonance that often exists between a historian's intellectual goals and personal commitments.

In completing this book I have received invaluable support and assistance from the Rassweiler and Bek families, especially Anne's husband John and her daughter Janet, and Anna Bek's grandson Evgeny Konstantinovich Andrusevich. I am also indebted to Russian-speaking friends for their assistance with some tricky questions of translation; Sarra Mebel, whose long and productive life as a scientist in the Soviet Union echoes Anna Bek's in some ways, has been particularly helpful. For transliterating the original Russian I used the standard Library of Congress system for the notes and bibliography, but in the interests of readability I simplified the spelling of names of people and places in the main text, for example, Evgeny instead of Evgenii, Ilina instead of Il'ina, and Tyumen instead of Tiumen'. Following Anne, I retained the Russian spelling of the surname Bek instead of changing it to the German Beck, since Dr. Evgeny Bek and his family, despite their German roots, were Russian by birth and culture. Anne's research in Siberia was supported by grants from the International Research and Exchanges Board in 1991 and the National Endowment for the Humanities (#RI-2076293) in 1993. Special thanks go to Anne's friend in Novosibirsk, Natasha Prittwitz, whose support was essential to her work. Finally, I would like to thank Janet Rabinowitch of Indiana University Press for making it possible to bring Anne's book to publication.

Adele M. Lindenmeyr

Chronology:
The Life of Anna Nikolaevna Zhukova-Bek

9 December 1869	Anna Nikolaevna Zhukova is born in Gornyi Zerentui, a mining settlement in the mining district of Nerchinsk Zavod, Transbaikal, to mine director Nikolai Mikhailovich Zhukov and Agrafena Afana-sevna Savinskaya.
1880	Family moves to Gugda mine.
1882	Enters high school at the Eastern Siberian Institute for Noble Girls in Irkutsk.
1888	Graduates from the Institute with highest honors, returns to Nerchinsk Zavod.
1894	Travels to St. Petersburg, enrolls in the Higher Women's Courses.
Summer 1895	Does famine relief work in a Tatar village in Ufa Province.
Fall 1895	Travels to France for medical education; after a brief stay in Paris, travels to Nancy.
1895–1897	Scientific and medical studies at the University in Nancy.
Summer 1897	Returns to Russia via Switzerland.
1897	Enters newly reopened Women's Medical Institute St. Petersburg.
1897–1903	Studies at Women's Medical Institute, St. Petersburg.
May 1901	Toward the end of her fourth year of study, is exiled from St. Petersburg home to Siberia for one year for leadership in student strike movement.

Summer 1901	Returns to Nerchinsk Zavod; begins working at local hospital, where she meets Dr. Evgeny Vladimirovich Bek (born 1865).
1901 or early 1902	Marries Dr. Bek.
1902	Her term of exile completed, returns to St. Petersburg to finish last year of medical school; first child born but dies in infancy.
1903	Graduates with distinction from Women's Medical Institute; returns to Nerchinsk Zavod.
1904–1905	The Beks serve in military hospitals at the front during the Russo-Japanese War.
1905–1906	Revolution in Russia; the Beks live in St. Petersburg while Dr. Bek studies surgery.
1906	Daughter Lyudmila (Lyusya) is born.
1906–1912	The Beks live in Aksha in Transbaikal, where Dr. Bek is physician for the Cossack Host of the region.
1909	Aksha Community Center opens, founded by Anna Nikolaevna.
1912–1923	The Beks live in Chita, where Anna Nikolaevna practices medicine and teaches science, physiology, and psychology, and directs evening courses for adults.
1914	Beginning of World War I; Dr. Bek is mobilized into the army.
1915	Dr. Bek dies of typhus contracted while treating Turkish prisoners of war.
February–March 1917	Revolution overthrows Russian monarchy; Provisional Government established.
October 1917	Bolshevik Party overthrows Provisional Government in Petrograd; Soviet state established.
1918–1920	Russian Civil War; Chita is headquarters of Cossack ataman and anti-Bolshevik commander Grigory Semenov.
1919	Serves as director of regional mental hospital in Chita.
1920	Red Army takes Chita, Soviet power returns.

1920–1922	Directs local government departments for the protection of motherhood and children in Chita; moves to Irkutsk with her daughter, Lyudmila.
1923–1930	Teaches psychology and pedology as a faculty member of the psychology department at the School of Education of Irkutsk University.
1925	Promoted to assistant professor (*dotsent*) of pedology.
1926	Daughter Lyudmila marries Konstantin Andrusevich.
1927	Promoted to head of pedology department at Irkutsk University.
1930	Moves to Novosibirsk, where daughter and family live, to become head of pedology research laboratory at the Institute of Communist Education and the Institute for the Protection of the Health of Children and Adolescents.
1931	Invited to Tomsk to head pedology department at the School of Education of Tomsk University (later renamed Tomsk Pedagogical Institute).
1932	Promoted to professor of pedology at Tomsk Pedagogical Institute.
1934	Under criticism for her political views and support of the now suspect discipline of pedology, submits her resignation from her professorship, goes on academic pension, and moves to Novosibirsk.
1934–1936	Heads the research laboratory in the department for the protection of children's health of the regional public health department, teaches psychology at the Evening Pedagogical Institute.
July 4, 1936	Communist Party Central Committee condemns pedology as a "pseudo-science" and requires pedologists to disavow the discipline publicly; Anna Nikolaevna fired from teaching psychology for refusing to do so.
1936 (or 1935)– 1942	Works as pediatrician at children's polyclinic in Novosibirsk.
1942–1943	Works as physician in industrial trade school in Novosibirsk.

1943–1944	Works as medical consultant at day care center on state farm where daughter and family live; moves in with daughter and family.
1948	Begins to write her memoirs.
1954	Dies at age eighty-four.

THE LIFE OF A
RUSSIAN WOMAN DOCTOR

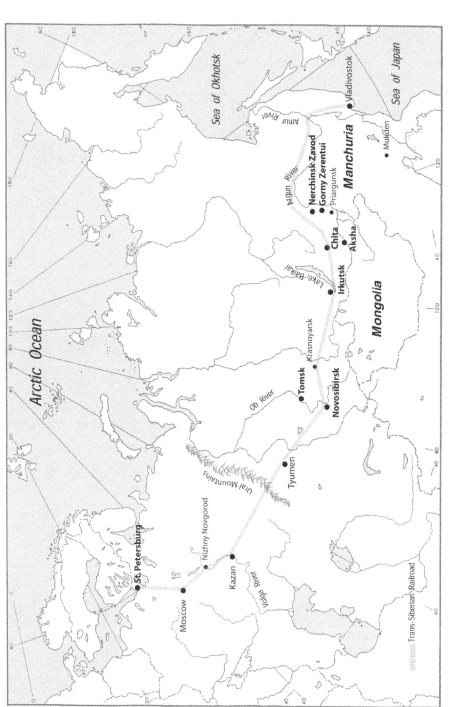

Anna Bek's Siberia

Introduction

A Journey to Siberia

Anne D. Rassweiler

Discovering Anna Nikolaevna Zhukova-Bek

In 1996 I became the first American historian to travel in the long-closed Siberian territories on the Chinese border, and the first American to visit the city of Chita since George Kennan, the nineteenth-century traveler and author of *Siberia and the Exile System* (1891).[1] I was on a mission of discovery and, like Kennan, found my mission broadened and changed as I traveled. My original goal was to follow the steps taken by the subject of my biographical study, the Siberian doctor and professor of psychology Anna Nikolaevna Zhukova-Bek. I first learned about Anna Nikolaevna in 1990 through her memoir. Her daughter, Lyudmila Evgenevna Andrusevich (1906–1995), gave me the as yet unpublished manuscript of the memoir, along with her own recollections, in response to an advertisement I ran in a newspaper in Novosibirsk, the capital of western Siberia, as I hunted for local memoirs of the revolutionary period. "My mother was an exceptional woman, you will want to read her memoirs," she kept repeating to me.

Born of Russian parents in 1869 in a tiny mining settlement east of Lake Baikal, Anna Nikolaevna grew up convinced that she could achieve an independent career. She became a doctor and a social activist battling for the education of adults and underprivileged children. She moved on to become a professor of psychology and child development, teaching in the major Siberian intellectual centers of Irkutsk, Tomsk, and Novosibirsk. Intrepid in her pursuit of a just society and intellectual honesty, she strove to understand and improve the world about her, and along the way challenged the tsarist military hierarchy, Marxist scholasticism, and the doctors' "old boy" networks. She died in 1954, having recorded the major events of her life in a memoir that was published in Russia only in 1996.[2]

Although Anna Nikolaevna was seventy-nine years old at the time she began writing and was confined to her bed by illness, her memoir reflects her courage and vigor. Her forthright commitment to intellectual development and her occasional flashes of laughter at herself won my interest and stimulated my desire to know more about her. As I translated the memoir I wondered about the places she described. Embarking on a journey to collect information about her, I followed her footsteps from the small mining towns where she was born and grew up; to Irkutsk, once known as the Paris of Siberia, where she had gone to school; to the Cossack areas bordering on China where she had worked; to Chita, the little-known capital of the Transbaikal, where she had taught, written, and served as president of boards and organizations; and to Novosibirsk, where she lived and worked in her final years. I traveled in areas known to Americans for their trackless, frozen wastelands, tsarist prison camps and the Soviet Gulag, and secret military installations. But in the summer Siberia blooms with wild peonies in white and pink, purple asters, and the golden jewel flower. The rolling steppes invite the rider; the brilliantly clear streams, the fisherman; the forests, the hiker, bird-watcher, and hunter. Summer vegetables, often starting and finishing in greenhouses, allure the hungry. Honey, berries, mushrooms, and pine nuts entice the fall traveler. The real natural beauty and traditional Siberian hospitality contradict our forbidding stereotypes of Siberia.

A Journey to Siberia

A glance at a map will suggest to you some of the difficulties I unthinkingly embraced when I resolved to visit the far-flung places where Anna Nikolaevna had lived and worked. Siberia is a vast territory of 2.5 million square miles, much larger than the People's Republic of China, twice the size of the United States (extending forty-three hundred miles from the Ural Mountains in the west to the eastern mountain ranges that divide Siberia from the Russian Far East), more than twice the size of European Russia, and inclusive of seven time zones. How do you get from here to there—if *here* is the western Siberian city of Novosibirsk, and *there* is Chita, located east of Lake Baikal and just north of the border with Mongolia, or the small towns Nerchinsk Zavod or Aksha, both within three hundred miles of Chita but in opposite directions! Where do you stay when you *get* there? And how do you go about obtaining the information I was looking for?

Wondrous things happen, that's how. Chivalry and family honor motivated Anna Nikolaevna's grandson, Evgeny Konstantinovich Andrusevich, to take my trip in hand. He had visited Transbaikal the previous year in preparation for the publication in 1996 of the book containing his grandfather's medical dissertation and his grandmother's memoir. When he learned of my plan to visit the distant towns where his grandmother had spent half her life, he decided he had to help me. "A woman alone, she'll never get there," he exclaimed; "It is my duty to help a foreigner, especially a woman alone. I also have an obligation to my grandmother to help someone interested in her work."

One might ask why I was embarking on this journey "in the footsteps of Anna Nikolaevna." Who was she, and what was her appeal to me? To begin with there was her lively memoir. She wrote in a large hand in lined notebooks like the ones schoolchildren use. She included extracts from a childhood diary, notes she made on the process of aging as she observed it in herself, and poems she wrote on her child's birth and her husband's death. Her words gave life to places, people, and events. By choosing her topics and omitting others, she shaped her legacy, her story for the reader. Her memoir reflects her personality, her desires and dislikes, her moods and humors. And I found additional texts reflecting Anna Nikolaevna's professional and personal interests: articles she wrote on sex education, social behavior, and very young children; political speeches; and letters to a friend.

Most important to me as a historian, a biographer, and a woman was Anna Nikolaevna's life and how she chose to live it in her own way. She dared to dream of becoming a doctor, even if it meant leaving her small mining town of Nerchinsk Zavod to travel more than four thousand miles to St. Petersburg, and thence to France for her education. All her life she worked for what she believed was right. Anna Nikolaevna did not settle for the conventional marriage that would have pleased her father but sought her own adult life course. Her marriage to Dr. Evgeny Vladimirovich Bek (1865–1915) was a loving partnership between two professionals dedicated to improving the health and welfare of their fellow Siberians. In addition to working with him in remote public health clinics, she opened schools to teach illiterate adults, young children, and children with learning difficulties. Unlike the Kerenskys and Stalins of her generation she did not lead governments but fought for evolutionary change in society, professional autonomy, and progress in the classroom. But Anna Nikolaevna was not shy about challenging the Establishment. She led student protests against the tsarist government, publicly denounced military officers, criticized the claims of senior doctors in medical associations, and argued with Communist Party officials about their educational assumptions.

Anna Nikolaevna's life also seemed to reflect the distinctive character and spirit often attributed to Russians from Siberia. Except for the few years that she spent in St. Petersburg and France pursuing her education, she lived her entire life in Siberia. Ever since the nineteenth century observers have characterized Russian Siberians as different from their brothers and sisters west of the Urals, more independent and broader in their thinking. Some, like the twentieth-century Siberian patriot and writer Valentin Rasputin, have argued that the very landscape stimulated their strength and independence:

> In view of nature's greatness and unabating triumph, human beings could not help feeling strong and significant, and the sparseness of population reinforced this outlook. The gigantic efforts they expended in order to tighten their hold and to survive in this rugged land made them inclined to respect themselves, as if they stood just as tall as everything about them, even taller. The whole world alongside them breathed an austere dignity and freedom, a concealed depth and strength, and in its outward tranquility a concealed tension could be sensed; Siberians,

quite naturally, adopted this spirit, and, when superimposed on their ancestors' elemental love of liberty, it became set.[3]

Rasputin also suggests that the immigrant origins of the Russian Siberian population profoundly shaped Siberian history and identity. First explored by traders and adventurers, Siberia attracted ambitious men in search of military glory and riches derived from furs, gold, and silver. They were joined by land-hungry peasants, who migrated from European Russia seeking farmland and freedom. Siberia's distinctive character also resulted from its use as a vast outdoor prison by the tsarist monarchy from the seventeenth century. Convicts sent into Siberian exile ranged from runaway serfs, peasant rebels, and common criminals to political opponents such as the Decembrists, the novelist Fyodor Dostoevsky, Polish revolutionaries, and socialists of all stripes. One of Anna Nikolaevna's own ancestors was a Cossack from the Don region exiled to Siberia for his participation in the Pugachev uprising of 1771–73.[4]

Finally, I felt that there were parallels between Anna Nikolaevna and me. I shared her desire for personal freedom, the drive to achieve change through education, and even her occasional self-righteousness. I liked her youthful courage and tenacity, her commitment to her professional training, and her sense of humor. Her actions drew me to her, this intrepid woman who challenged conventional paths. Her life story spurred my interest in writing women's history—recording, thinking about, and commenting on women's life goals and activities. Now I would actually step into her past, guided by her grandson.

Novosibirsk

I arrived in Novosibirsk, the large industrial capital of western Siberia, during one of the few dark hours of a Siberian summer, at 2:30 A.M. on 15 June 1996. My home base was a friend's apartment in Akademgorodok, a town just south of Novosibirsk, where the Siberian Division of the Russian Academy of Sciences is located. In Siberia, a friend does not allow a visiting friend to arrive unmet, even in the dark hours before dawn. The son-in-law of a friend of this friend came to find me and whisk me to my welcome in Akademgorodok: a breakfast with my friends of the last decade. Over *bliny* (Russian pancakes), fresh strawberries, cream, and tea we caught up on the time that had passed since my last visit three years earlier. On the following day I met my future traveling companion for the first time. Evgeny Konstantinovich and his wife, Zinaida Anatolevna, entertained me at a formal meal in their living room, and toasted my upcoming trip with vodkas he had flavored with nuts and two kinds of berries, *cheryomukha* and *ryabina,* that gave special flavors and, in one case, a rosy hue. A good-looking man with a beautiful carriage and an energetic manner, Evgeny Konstantinovich explained, "I have been to Chita and Aksha. I have met people there, and I will be able to help you." He had contacted relations he had met and persons connected with his grandmother's life in order to tell them that I was coming. He had written to museums and state archives where I might search out additional materials.

We began with a visit to the cemetery where Anna Nikolaevna is buried—a large, crowded wooded lot north of Novosibirsk. Here, at the end of her journey, I was just beginning mine. At the cemetery Evgeny Konstantinovich invited me to join him in a ritual to honor her memory. "Come join us, have a *ryumochka,* a little glass of vodka. Here, have a slice of bread and tomato. We're honoring Anna Nikolaevna, she died fifty-four years ago today. See, she's buried here with her daughter and son-in-law—he died the same year that she did. There they are inside this blue-painted iron grill fence where we're sitting, with their names so elegantly carved in gold on the marble stones. Incidentally, we had trouble fitting in my mother, Anna Nikolaevna's daughter. The authorities said there was no room in the plot, but, you know, ten thousand rubles here and there—in our new crazy money—we found someone who said: 'Caskets crumble with time, we'll just slide the daughter in here on the side; there will be room for them all together.'

"We don't raise our glasses in toasts in *pominki,* this ceremony of remembrance, we just drink our glass down and think about the person, her life and interests, her role in our lives," Evgeny Konstantinovich continued. "I wonder what she'd think of our being here, thinking and talking about her. Do you suppose she hears us, is her spirit about? You know, she didn't believe in God, she was a Marxist, a materialist. But she always felt the spirit of her husband after he died, she felt particularly close to him then—even closer than when he was alive because then he was always so busy with his work. She describes this in the memoirs you'll be reading. And late in her memoir writing, when she put down some of her reflections on life, she ruminated on the dual nature, the spiritual and material quality of the universe, on the conservation of energy and spirit as well as the conservation of material. She recognized that materialists, who insisted on the primacy of material things, 'may move from their continued study of the laws of nature to the study of creative energy in nature, that is, to what is called god.' That was a long way from what she was thinking as a revolutionary in 1901, when she was suspended from medical school for leading a student demonstration and was exiled to Siberia. Well," her grandson concluded, "she was always exploring ideas, as well as acting in so many different spheres—she was quite a woman!"

Moving forward in time we next visited the places where she had lived and worked in Novosibirsk: a children's clinic and a kindergarten at an experimental state stock farm.[5] The clinic now serves abusers of alcohol and drugs, and the kindergarten no longer exists—the state and the farm have no money. All that remains of the building is the foundation. All that remains of the state farm is the name and a few old pensioners. The land is being eaten up by "new Russians" who build two-story summer houses equipped with indoor plumbing and multiple electrical appliances. We visited the old barrack apartment where the family lived in the 1940s and found a young man there, defended by two large Rottweilers. Family bedrooms and living space had become a fur atelier. The young man was hustling to make elegant hats and stylish collars, while watching Western videos on a large television. He was the new breed of Russian: working for personal profit, enjoying the fruits of his labors behind a fortified iron door, and at the same time very hospitable to the casual strangers who knocked and asked to come in. How surprised Anna Nikolaevna would have been at this use of her quarters.

"We are not going to stay in hotels, Anna Livingstonovna," Evgeny Konstantinovich had written me, inventing a Russian patronymic for me from my father's first name. "They are too dangerous, especially for foreigners, and too expensive." Evgeny Konstantinovich often expressed current Russian worldviews: life is dangerous for solitary women, who are not particularly capable in the public domain because they are simply women; strangers to a locale, especially foreign strangers, cannot accomplish much because they do not know who holds local power; crime is increasing today and is often directed at foreigners and business people who have cash and valuables; and conventional skirt lengths are prettier than either very long or very short! As we traveled he learned that I speak Russian, have developed know-how in Russian culture and in archival and museum politics and procedures, and that people react positively to that. We often discussed our cultures and learned from each other as we went along.

Irkutsk

We first traveled to Irkutsk, the prosperous capital of eastern Siberia. Anna Nikolaevna had attended boarding school there in the 1880s and had returned in the 1920s to teach at the university.[6] Evgeny Konstantinovich had requested lodging from Lyudmila Fortunatovna Moskalenko, a woman with a very special connection to Anna Nikolaevna and especially to her husband, Dr. Evgeny Vladimirovich Bek. The Beks had sponsored her gifted but impecunious mother who went on to become a medical doctor and university professor. She remained close to the Beks throughout their lives, and kept up with Anna Nikolaevna's family after her mother died. "Of course I want to welcome your American professor," she wrote in response to Evgeny Konstantinovich's request. "I'm sending you the plan of my apartment. If you think it would not be too modest for her, please come and make yourselves at home here." She sent a sketch, showing a single room for me, opening onto a hall, and then the bathroom, the kitchen, and the living room, with her room adjoining the living room. She gave up her room to my guide and slept on the living room couch.

Lyudmila Fortunatovna herself met us at the airport and recruited a son to drive us about Irkutsk. She made innumerable phone calls to help us in locating people and institutions, and worried about us if we were late coming home from research appointments. Whenever we did arrive, there were sliced tomatoes and cucumbers from the garden and a special thick sour cream available only in the summer. There were home-grown potatoes, pickles, jams, and other conserves. And there was wine and, after we ate, songs about Baikal, the steppes, and a lonely escaped prisoner wandering in the Transbaikal wilderness.

We saw the Institute for Noble Girls, founded in Irkutsk in 1845, from which Anna Nikolaevna had graduated in 1888 with highest honors. Now part of the university, it houses the mathematics and physics departments. Green computer screens flicker where once young girls studied French and German, and learned to curtsey. We found a parquet floor in one classroom and decided that it belonged to the formal reception hall where Anna Nikolaevna had received her gold medal. Today it has rows of scruffy desks—one with the lyrics of Sergeant Pepper carved into the desk top, another with carvings of foul Russian curse words. Anna Nikolaevna returned to this very building in the 1920s when it came into the hands of the university's medical institute. She lived nearby, in the "White House," once home of Siberia's imperial administration, later an apartment building and now the university library. Her grandson, Evgeny Konstantinovich, was born in that building, so of course we had to pay a visit. The bibliographer who ruled the top floor invited us in to see Anna Nikolaevna's former apartment with its huge Russian stove. Two young men at desks in the apartment barely raised their heads at our invasion of their space. They went right on entering bibliographical data into their computers while we tried to imagine the shapes and contours of Evgeny Konstantinovich's birthplace, seventy years earlier.

We had much less luck with documents. We visited a new city museum and found it still in the paint-and-paper stage, all its collections in boxes and unavailable. But the assistant director loaned me her copy of an 1895 report on the Institute for Noble Girls where I read details of the school's first fifty years, its mission to promote women's education, its directors and graduates. On visiting the state archives we learned that all the files on Anna Nikolaevna had been moved to the medical institute. The archive at the medical institute was closed, an impressive bulky iron lock in the hasp of its plain sheet metal door. The archivist, like most university professors and staff, had received no salary after the university ran out of funds in the spring. The same was true of museum staff. Most professionals had left on summer-long unpaid vacations.

Chita

We had completed our first steps in the East. We boarded a local sleeper for our next destination, Chita, the capital city of Chita Province. At about 4:30

A.M. the train conductor collected our berth linen, and at 5:00 we arrived. Here, in Chita, Anna Nikolaevna had lived for more than ten years, seeing patients, doing research in medicine and pedagogy, founding schools, and serving in numerous professional and community organizations.[7] She was in Chita when World War I broke out, and she saw her husband die of typhus. During the Russian civil war in 1918–1920, which followed the Bolshevik Revolution, she defended Bolshevik refugees from the Whites and safeguarded newly bought democratic schoolbooks from the anti-Bolshevik Semenov's rogue army. Here she brought up and educated her daughter, Lyudmila (born in 1906), and struggled to keep her in school when the young girl wanted to marry. I was planning to wander through the old sections of the town to see where she lived and to visit the museum and state archives. I was also planning to interview a ninety-year-old woman who had known Anna Nikolaevna many years ago.

But where would we stay? Our Irkutsk hostess had sent us off with a letter to her nephew, Stanislav, a priest—or at least the son of a first cousin, which essentially made him a nephew. Lyudmila Fortunatovna knew he had a city apartment that he was not using; he was living at his dacha for the summer. We could not telephone him because he had no home phone. There was a phone in the church where he served as priest, but it could not be used for personal business. The letter introduced us, my scholarly quest, and our request for lodging. Our second possibility was to visit Evgeny Konstantinovich's niece—also "essentially" a niece. She had invited us by phone and said she would work something out when we arrived. However, she lived an hour from the city in a suburb served by infrequent public transportation, an obstacle to making appointments and doing research. Further, she had a very small apartment, and we would seriously crowd her and her husband. Alternatively she would lodge us in the Home for the Elderly, where she was the director. Well, that would certainly be different. I noticed that I was getting to be of that age for, passing as a Russian "pensioner," I traveled free on most Russian buses, and young people stood up to offer me a seat.

Evgeny Konstantinovich left me in the waiting room of the Chita train station at 5:00 A.M. Five hours later he returned triumphantly. He had found Father Stanislav, who reported that his apartment was unlivable, but he had found a parishioner who would be delighted to welcome us to his apartment. The man and his wife and granddaughter, in town for the granddaughter's christening, were living at their dacha, with only the daughter in the three-room apartment. They were happy to give us shelter. They insisted we feel at home, fed us, and wished me every success in my work.

The word *dacha* should not conjure up images of luxurious or quaint summer residences or cottages near a forest brook, lake, or orchard. Most Siberians have a small hut or half of a one-room log house plastered and white-washed inside, with a small wood stove for heat. Water is from a well or village pump, the outhouse is at the back of the garden, and cooking is done in the summer kitchen, a nearby shed. One lives there in the summer to sow, harvest, and preserve the vegetables, especially potatoes and fruits, which will sustain family and friends through the winter. In addition, life at the dacha provides the fresh air and clear sunshine that city dwellers are deprived of by the toxic smog that hangs over Chita and cities like it. From the dacha there are excursions to the woods and rivers—not all the time is spent working; the high point of the week is when the bathhouse fire is lit, and its room becomes steamy from the water thrown on the metal stove or piles of hot stones. Family and guests take their turns steaming themselves, chatting, beating one another with whisks made from freshly cut, sweetly scented birch twigs or stinging nettles, and washing away the cares of the week.

From our apartment in the heart of Chita, we easily found the museum and archives. State archive staff and Raisa Ivanovna Tsuprik, a well-known bibliographer in Chita, had prepared materials on Anna Nikolaevna and her husband, and quickly helped us prepare our formal requests for admittance, brought materials, and copied those needed. They even invited other readers to take a day off so they could devote themselves exclusively to serving us.[8]

But we could not spend all our time in research. I had some visa formalities to attend to. We walked to the militia station. There was a line forming, which we successfully circumvented by entering through a different door. I wrote my supplication to the officer of the day, requesting permission to register in the city and to travel to the small village of Aksha, southwest of Chita, and the town of Nerchinsk Zavod, southeast of Chita. (In the old days, which ended only in 1991, these requests would have been turned down as unthinkable, as the destinations were too close to the Chinese border.) But my supplication was winningly worded, with Evgeny Konstantinovich's creative suggestions and his corrections of my grammar and spelling. The handsome major read it through, her smile broadening as she read. I had written in part:

> I am making a trip through towns of Siberia with the goal of collecting materials for writing a book on women in Siberia. In the course of my travels I will visit museums and libraries, and interview women who contributed to the development of culture and the maintenance of health in Siberia.
>
> From the USA citizen, Anne Rassweiler

"You are really studying and writing about Siberian women's history?" she asked, in some disbelief. I nodded. "Why do you want to write about this woman, Anna Nikolaevna?" I told her about this star in Chita's cultural history: she was a practicing doctor at a time when very few women were; she founded a museum and filled it with artifacts; she started schools and taught in them; and she conducted medical research and published it. I knew as I spoke that I cared that not only should people in Chita know about Anna Nikolaevna but that readers worldwide should become acquainted with her, and with women like her, women who spent their professional lives working to broaden popular access to health and education.

"Very well," the major said, raising her head from my application, "you may go. Have a successful trip." I thanked her, promised her a copy of my book, and exulted over the political changes in Russia that allowed me to travel where I chose.

Our next administrative task was to seek assistance in getting from here to there. We could get to Aksha by bus—the schedule suggested a four-hour trip (which, in fact, took seven hours)—but getting to Nerchinsk Zavod was not going to be easy. Evgeny Konstantinovich decided to confer with Dr. Vitaly Olegovich Flek, a professor at the Chita State Medical Academy who had a serious interest in the Beks' work. His institute was financing publication of the book containing Anna Nikolaevna's memoir and her husband's medical dissertation, a pioneering investigation into the etiology of a bone disease once widespread in eastern Siberia and still occasionally showing up there. Dr. Flek welcomed us into his office and shouted for someone to prepare coffee. He set up a table and added delicious chocolates while we talked about the forthcoming book and our shared interest in the Beks.

Turning to the troublesome question of the day, Evgeny Konstantinovich asked, "Would you be able to lend us a car?" After a few phone calls it was clear that the answer was no. No gas was available; one car was out of town, and two were in the shop; and there was no money for drivers, regardless of whether Dr. Flek requested funds from his own institute or from the hospital. The financial crunch that most officialdom in Russia was suffering was obviously shared here.

"Why not take the train?" We had considered that, but no train came close to Nerchinsk Zavod. Dr. Flek studied his list of institute graduates. "Excelsior!" his tone suggested. "Here in Priargunsk is one of our very best men! He'll get you from the end of the train line to the towns and museums that you want to visit." He tried to call this paragon but the phone no longer worked—a victim of the collapsing state infrastructure. "Well, never mind, don't worry, I'll get in touch with him and he'll take care of you." We thanked our latest provider and set off for our next objective: Aksha.

Aksha

Our bus moved along the river valleys and hills, through rolling steppe land and rising ridges. I thought about Anna Nikolaevna and her husband making this trip with horses. They traveled in September, but an early snowstorm had caught them in the hills. Anna Nikolaevna was traveling with a newborn, so the journey must have been very difficult. She was not impressed with the small town of Aksha and its limited intellectual life. But she and her husband left it a richer place. The townspeople loved them. Anna Nikolaevna and her husband, Evgeny Vladimirovich, saw patients everywhere in the region as well as in the town's hospital. They also founded a cultural center and museum, persuading wealthy cattlemen to donate money, hunters to provide skeletons and skins, and miners to give minerals and fossils, while the populace as a whole brought books, museum materials, and their talents to the schools, theater, and chorus.[9]

When we arrived in Aksha our host met us with his motorcycle. I addressed him by his name and patronymic, Alexander Alekseevich. Evgeny Konstantinovich had cautioned me: "It will do him honor." But he met me with a big hug, and said, "I am Sasha and this is my wife, Raya," as they bent Russian practice to make me feel at home. They welcomed us to a table laden with the fruits of the summer and their labor. We always ate well, thanks to Raya's skills, the garden, and the prolific cows. After dinner Sasha took us on a tour of the village and its environs. I sat in the sidecar or "carriage," as it is called in Russian. The next day he took us fishing in the river as well.

Sasha, too, was connected to the Beks. His grandfather had worked with Evgeny Vladimirovich as the village scribe. Evgeny Konstantinovich had written Sasha and Raya of my projected trip, and they invited us to stay with them. Their home is an unpainted, low wooden house with a tin roof. It has an entry area for the storage of food and work clothing, a small kitchen, narrow hall, and three rooms. The house is full of light and impeccably clean. Outside, within the courtyard, are the bathhouse, service shed for a motorcycle, water pump, garden, chicken house, pig sty, outhouse, and, beyond the first fence, a more extensive plot for potatoes and the cowshed where the calves are fed in the summer evenings and where the stock live in the winter.

Sometimes Sasha and Raya asked about issues that deeply troubled them. "Do you have alcoholism in America? Do women drink? Here the young women are beginning to drink." "What is going to happen to our young people? There are no jobs; there is no money for medicine, for teachers. Some schools are closing." They wondered what good a free market could bring, when the chicken factory had closed because it could not survive, yet small private stores were selling imported chickens. As jobs disappeared, money for goods was scarce and there was an increase in crime. I could only listen and sympathize, and hope that the concrete factory that the Chinese were building would open soon.

The villagers of Aksha welcomed us as honored guests. Albina Georgievna Shchalpegina, the director of the museum, offered us a tour, including a video made by Chita's television station about the history of the Beks. She had a cameraman, her son Evgeny, ready so that they could add a clip about us to the original tape. She went with us to see the house where the Beks had lived. The residents invited us in, and we tried to imagine what it was like years ago. The local newspaper interviewed us, and then its editor and her husband entertained us with a cookout at a nearby lake where the district's chief administrator joined us. The main course was imported American chicken legs, first called "*nozhki Busha*" or "Bush's legs" after the first President Bush, and now imported from Clinton's Arkansas. Our hosts were for "reform" as they defined it. "Yes, we are for the market system and economic freedom," Velyamir Alekseevich Stambulov, the district administrator, said. He and the editor between them had six small stores selling foreign goods and alcohol. Although they had voted for President Yeltsin in both elections in the 1990s, they were concerned about the voracious demands made by the central government. "They send us nothing, no money for schoolteachers or hospital workers [both of whom were on strike locally], no money for pension payments. We have nothing to invest in rebuilding our factories or farms. The center takes all our taxes, and no local industry can succeed because the center taxes everything to death." We continued to talk politics and economics while the vodka held out.

All too soon it was time to go. We left Aksha with a sense of what it had been like ninety years ago when the Beks had made it their home. People knew and know one another. Then, as now, it did "take a village to raise a child." We were laden with gifts from our new friends' homes—their lush tomatoes, home-baked breads, and honey. Evgeny Konstantinovich received a wonderful promise from the chief administrator. The new hospital would be named in honor of his grandfather, Dr. Evgeny Vladimirovich Bek.

Nerchinsk Zavod

Once back in Chita we left the bus for the train and plunged ahead into the night and into the unknown. Dr. Flek had promised to telephone "one of our best men" in Priargunsk, the last stop on the railway line and the jumping-off spot for the silver mines and for Nerchinsk Zavod in particular, where Anna Nikolaevna had spent part of her youth.[10] To our great pleasure Dr. Yakov Mikhailovich Ponikov, a very handsome dark-haired Cossack, was there to meet us. A psychiatrist and head of the hospital, he took us to his home where his equally handsome wife, Marina Leonidovna, also a psychiatrist, fed us a substantial breakfast while we discussed alternative plans. Dr. Ponikov recommended that we drive to "Nerzavod" and visit the museum to see what we could learn; then visit nearby Gornyi Zerentui, where Anna Nikolaevna was born, and visit the museum there as well; and finally race back to sleep in his comfortable home. If necessary, he added, we could adjust our plans and find beds through the local doctor. We were not to worry about arranging an overnight stay ahead of time, he assured us.

Siberians welcome guests; it is a privilege to have company in one's home. In Siberian tradition the host's honor is at stake. Siberians feed guests with the best provisions they have, entertain them, and seek to help them in every way possible. Everywhere I went I was privileged to be so received.

Dr. Ponikov's wonderful driver skirted great gullies and holes in local roads and sped along the main road. He stopped for good views, interesting wildflowers, and a medicinal spring. He skirted a drunk fast asleep on the warm macadam as well as free-roaming horses, cows, goats, and fowl.

Our first encounter in Nerchinsk Zavod was providential. We came upon a short stocky man with oddly bent arms and legs, a textbook example of the local disease the Beks had studied and photographed. He graciously chatted with us, telling us that the disease was disappearing. People refrained from using the stream water that carries harmful minerals, as the Beks hypothesized, or possibly bacteria that skew calcification processes, although the actual pathology of the disease was still not firmly established.

We passed the hospital where Dr. Ponikov had announced our arrival and went on to visit the museum where the very new young guide was reading up on the Beks so she could make an official presentation. We were soon joined by the hospital's chief doctor. We conferred, asking if there was anyone in town who might remember the Drs. Bek or Anna Nikolaevna's father's family. Speeding away in his ambulance, the doctor soon returned to lead us to a small log house where one of the town's oldest citizens lived, a man of ninety-two. But he could offer no help. He told us, "I don't remember. I was concussed in the war and I don't remember anything."

We climbed a precipitous road to get an overview of the town. We could see the hospital, museum, and, to my surprise, the house where the renowned modernist painter Vasily Kandinsky was born, a building taller than its neighbors with large columns framing its front door. On our return the doctor's driver escorted us to an empty cafeteria where dinner had been prepared. "But don't drink the local vodka," he said, giving us cans of Finnish vodka, "you can't be sure what's in it." Our energies restored, we toured on with our guides to Gornyi Zerentui, the mining settlement where Anna Nikolaevna was born and whose dangers she so devastatingly described in her memoir. The efficient doctor found the volunteer who is the caretaker of the museum and brought her to us, but she could do nothing. The great lock on the museum door had been so battered by vandals that she couldn't put the key into the keyhole. Its icons had just been stolen—hence the great lock. She invited us to spend our available time with her and offered dinner or tea. She would have been chagrined, even insulted, had we refused, so we went to visit her home and yard, met her husband, and left carrying her gift of home-smoked fatback, a Russian delicacy.

Our doctor and his driver escorted us to where our paths would diverge as we headed home. There at the crossroads they laid out tasty morsels salvaged from our dinner and filled small glasses in a traditional *pososhok* or "one for the road." Learning at dinner that I was interested in old coins, the doctor gave me a beautiful souvenir of coins minted in Nerzavod in the days of Catherine II. We drank a farewell toast and drove back to Priargunsk.

The Return Journey

Our brief stay in Priargunsk was filled with the contrasts that characterize post-Soviet times. The home of our hosts, the Drs. Ponikov, was the most luxurious we visited. The kitchen had more appliances than I have seen elsewhere, a number imported from Germany, and the refrigerator and stove were in mint condition. The Ponikovs had purchased new wallpaper to hang, and they urged us to return in the coming year to see its beauty. With the salaries of two specialists, Yakov Ponikov told me, "We live very well in normal times, but no one is being paid now, not us, not the hospital workers, and not the people who come to us needing medical care."

Their daughter, Anya, took us on a tour of Priargunsk. At seventeen she is as thin as her style-conscious peers around the world and, like many, dresses in slim jeans and a tank top. She is entering a three-year economics program "which I can do in a year" and is planning to take a similar law program, encouraged by her father. "But," she says, "I would really like to study English and come to America." Anya took us along the main street of Priargunsk and down its cross-street. This is not a populous area; it was a military outpost with greater importance in the Stalinist period than now. We saw Lenin still standing in the Park of Rest and Culture. The former department store was now a collection of poor little private enterprise countertops. We walked down to the market, a haven for Chinese traders laying out their bargain clothing, goods, and watery greenhouse tomatoes. Later that evening Dr. Ponikov expressed his concern. "About what?" I asked. "That there will be blood," he answered, worried about the growing rift between the rich and the poor. "The free market system is fine, in principal," he argued, "but it came too fast with no protection, no help for those who weren't able to make it right away. Now there is no money for them, for schools, medicines, or pensions."

All too soon it was time to hurry to catch the train back to Chita. Dr. Ponikov alerted the conductor to the presence of friends. She responded with great solicitude for our comfort, bringing us tea and a blanket as the nights were getting cool. We waved good-bye to the Ponikovs and headed back to the city of Chita. Our final days there were filled to the brim with reviewing useful documents unearthed by archival staff, making and collecting copies, granting interviews on television about the Beks, continuing my research, and recording my impressions of Chita. A distant relative of Evgeny Konstantinovich invited us to dine. She was dabbling "in trade," suspect as that phrase is to most Siberians, and was building a two-story house with indoor plumbing, a living room with a fireplace, and a large master bedroom with a balcony. The family took us mushrooming, as they had learned that I am an ardent mycophile, and also to visit a pure spring whose water is good for whatever ails you. We picked a good evening to do this; Chita's water supply was shut off while muddy water was filtered out of the system. We went armed with old vodka bottles and larger containers. On the twenty-second day of our trans-Siberian journey, these distant relatives drove us to the airport for our flight to Novosibirsk.

My days in Novosibirsk were filled with appointments related to other research matters. I spent time looking at modest businesses whose owners need help to enter the market. I looked especially at enterprises headed by women. I feel a particular tie to them through my research on the history of Siberian women in the 1920s, when the Communists' women's department spearheaded a campaign for women's emancipation from the domination of men, the swamp of household tasks, illiteracy, and lack of worldly knowledge. The Communists promised women economic independence through job training and promotions. But the promised support networks did not materialize. I had seen a similar scenario in 1991, when Russian society promised women an end to their double burden of work and home care. Yet today they comprise more than 60 percent of the local unemployed, while state-supported child and medical care have all but disappeared and sexual exploitation and violence have increased. Those who want to win their independence and establish themselves as businesswomen interested me. They, like Anna Nikolaevna, challenge the conventions of how women *should* act.

As I traveled the vast distances I learned to appreciate the Siberian's cool about distance. I lived the life of the small village and town, and acquainted myself with the old Russian Siberian culture. Having visited the places where Anna Nikolaevna had lived and worked, and collected archival materials on the schools, museums, and other institutions she helped to establish, I better understood her life and her contributions as an educator, social reformer, and partner to her physician husband. Her memoir tells us much about what it meant to be Siberian, and about the vast social changes that occurred both before the revolution and during the first decades of the Soviet period. Finally, it demonstrates how political repression and academic conformity in the 1930s ended the period of revolutionary hope and experimentation in the 1920s, along with Anna Nikolaevna's own career.

At the same time I had a close look at the strains in Siberian society today. Every day I saw continuities with traditional Russian culture and Soviet practice, and the new sharp-edged challenges of post-Soviet market society. As I think about my travels in Anna Nikolaevna's land with the Siberian descendants of her family and friends, I recognize my own, similar desire for independence and our shared appreciation of the Siberian land and people.

A fitting finish to my journey in the steps of Anna Nikolaevna, guided by her grandson, was a holiday camping trip on the shore of the Ob Sea, the very large lake created by the damming of the Ob River. Friends and Bek descendants spent a few days hunting berries and mushrooms, swimming, and playing chess. We fished and cooked the fish we caught. We drank wine and sang songs. We swam in the early morning and late in the evening with the sun still visible at 10:00 P.M. A little cool crept into the air as August began and we folded our tents into neat packages for another day. I packed my bags for the last time. It may have been the beginning of Siberia's ten months of winter, and yet I would always remember that the entire rest of the year is summer, summer, and more summer! And I would also recall that the hearts and hospitality of Siberians keep you warm all year round.

Interpreting Anna Nikolaevna's Memoir

Anna Nikolaevna began writing her memoir in 1948, when she was old and bedridden with arthritis, in response to a request from her brother, Innokenty. She wrote, she says, for her daughter and grandsons. The selves she chose to present include the professor respected and loved by her students, and the scholar with a distinguished published record of research. She is also the woman who triumphed over odds to break out of a conventional mode, achieving an intellectual and public career. As she moved along in her writing, she began to include more personal matters—young loves, ironic amusement at some of her own actions, anger with unprofessional colleagues, and, most poignantly, the love she bore for the husband she so admired.

She leaves out a great deal that we would like to know, particularly her reflections on crucial events in her life and on the political revolutions swirling about her. For example, she recalls how she believed that she could have saved her mother's life, and later the life of her sister-in-law, had she possessed the medical knowledge, but she never mentions the death of her first baby from diarrhea and dehydration or her lack of intervention when her husband died from a tracheal block while recovering from typhus. She recalls her participation in a student strike in 1901 and her battles with tsarist officers during the Russo-Japanese War of 1904–1905, but she never discusses political events thereafter: not the revolution or civil war, the intra-party struggles of the Communist Party (to which she did not belong) in the 1920s, the forced industrialization and collectivization in the 1930s, or the Terror. Like most inhabitants of the Soviet Union in the 1930s, Anna Nikolaevna personally felt the impact of the repressions of the late 1930s, a time known as the Great Terror: her own brother was arrested, and her daughter and son-in-law, their belongings all packed, waited during the long nights, expecting to be arrested at any time. During this period her home was often filled with relatives on their way to and from labor camps or starving cities or domestic crises. The hard times women in Siberia endured during World War II and the lean years immediately following are also left out of her memoir. She says almost nothing about her own financial and living conditions, or the poverty and dependence to which her meager pension condemned her in old age. It is important to note in this context that Anna Nikolaevna lived her whole life under the threat of police scrutiny, first by the tsar's secret police and later by the watchguards of the Communist Party. When she wrote in the late 1940s and early 1950s, it was the latter, more pervasive and cruel of these police authorities that she had to consider, and perhaps she censored her words to ensure the life of her story. The once very political student activist became apolitical, and we must rely on speculation as to why this happened.

No less important to our understanding of Anna Nikolaevna's writing is that she was a woman who lived in an era of conflicting expectations of women, which she probably not only experienced internally but also with regard to her family and public life. Does she omit the birth and death of her first baby because she thinks that it will not be of interest to her grandsons? Or does she do so because she blamed herself as a mother or because such matters do not have a place in the story of a social activist and scholar? It was not uncommon among women revolutionaries and communist activists to bear and lose babies in the difficult circumstances of their lives, but usually they at least mentioned the fact. She writes little about her personal feelings toward family and friends: nothing of her struggle against her daughter's marriage and later her own family cares; her multiple services to her married daughter, whose children experienced nearly fatal accidents and illnesses; or the pleasure she took in her grandchildren. At the same time she devotes considerable space and attention to her feelings for her beloved husband, especially in the pieces she wrote after she finished the main text of her memoir, even including verses she wrote when he died.

At the same time this book yields rich insights into the lives of an entire generation of women who lived at a time of revolutionary change, extraordinary challenges, and unprecedented opportunities. Written in a lively and compelling style, Anna Nikolaevna's memoir reveals not only the experiences but also the motives and values of women who sought education, independence, and self-sufficiency, the obstacles they encountered and the influences of other women and men on their lives. Unlike the published memoirs of other women of the revolutionary and early Soviet period, which come from parts of Russia west of the Urals, *The Life of a Russian Woman Doctor* reveals the special context of Siberian geography and history—its population of emigrants, exiles, and convicts, the vast distances and isolation, the closeness and interdependence of families and communities, and the appreciation of nature. This book offers a rewarding excursion into Siberian social history and, no less important, an intimate acquaintance with an exceptional person of great charm and courage.

1.

Growing Up in the Transbaikal

In chapter 1 we meet Anna Nikolaevna's parents and large family of siblings and aunts, and learn about social and cultural expectations, limitations, and opportunities that came with growing up female in eastern Siberia. Born in 1869, Anna Nikolaevna spent her early childhood in the mining settlement of Gornyi Zerentui, one of the many mines spread out through the hills of the Nerchinsk District. The operation of such mines and living conditions for both management and workers come vividly to life in a piece she wrote after finishing her memoirs, "Reminiscences of Life on the Taiga Mine, Gugda," which is inserted here into chapter 1 of the memoirs. Anna Nikolaevna, from the age of seven to thirteen, lived at the Gugda gold mine with her family. She recalls the loneliness and lack of culture at the mining settlement. This isolation had contributed to her father obtaining a job there. Trained engineers refused to serve in distant posts where there were no amenities, so "practicals," men with experience but who lacked degrees in higher education, were promoted to manager to fill such posts. Anna Nikolaevna's father's official position as manager qualified him as a civil servant and entitled him to all the benefits attached to that status.[1]

The family seems not to have been impressed with the housing they received, suggesting that it had been better elsewhere. Certainly an indoor toilet was still an urban luxury and one not available in Gugda. Tanya, at fifteen, was responsible for the housework, leaving her mother free to take care of the younger children and the garden. Mother and Father both probably worried about raising their three daughters in this rough mining environment, where there were many men, lots of alcohol, and a wild atmosphere. Many miners were vagrants without names, either intentionally because they were hiding from the law or because they had legitimately forgotten them; hence there was Ivan Without-a-father and Ivan I-don't-remember. They were heavy drinkers and usually drank until their money ran out when work ended in the fall. This left them very poor in the face of oncoming winter and also in need of a continuing relationship with the mine to ensure future funds.

Chapter 1 also tells the story of Anna Nikolaevna's quest to pursue her education. One of the best-known schools in Siberia was the Eastern Siberian Institute for Noble Girls, opened in Irkutsk in 1845. The course of study there included mathematics, world and Russian history and geography, grammar, language and literature, French and German, and "the necessary and the newest information" in natural history and physics, calligraphy, drawing, handwork, dancing, singing, and music. This was the school that Anna

Nikolaevna entered at the age of thirteen—an imposing, even forbidding classical building near the Angara River. In this section of her memoirs she recounts the great influence of a progressive school inspector in the midst of the conservative official milieu that surrounded the school, and the clandestine reading of progressive literature. Six years later, in 1888, Anna Nikolaevna graduated with highest honors and returned home.

After Anna Nikolaevna returned home from Irkutsk her family moved closer to the town of Nerchinsk Zavod, to the Lopatikha mine. Living closer to town they could shop and attend events there. Nerchinsk Zavod, the administrative and cultural center of the district, was a small town founded in 1764 with approximately three thousand inhabitants at the time Anna Nikolaevna was growing up. It had a hospital, a pharmacy, and a public library. A school for children of white-collar workers taught writing, arithmetic, geometry, and drawing. A school for mine-surveying prepared graduates for mining and associated mountain jobs. The population in the outlying areas, namely, the people working in the mines and factories such as the one Anna Nikolaevna's father managed, came to Nerchinsk Zavod for amenities and culture.

The town had its own elite of engineers, factory owners, and merchants. Some of these became very successful financially and traveled widely. Some studied in St. Petersburg and Moscow, and received advanced degrees in the sciences and humanities. Some promoted liberal causes in spite of their financial dependence on the tsar and his agents. One of these was the wealthy merchant Vasily Silvestrovich Kandinsky, whose two-story home still stands in Nerchinsk Zavod; his son, Vasily, was the renowned modernist painter. The elder Kandinsky lent assistance to exiled Russian and Polish political prisoners. Another merchant family, the Butins, accumulated a magnificent fortune through their mining and trading enterprises, enabling family members to travel frequently to China, America, and Europe. At the Paris Exhibition in 1878 Mikhail Butin bought the largest mirror in existence at that time. He shipped it around the world and installed it in his glorious mansion, which George Kennan described as

> a superb private residence with hardwood marquetry floors, silken curtains, hangings of delicate tapestry, stained-glass windows, splendid chandeliers, soft Oriental rugs, white-and-gold furniture upholstered with satin, old Flemish paintings, marble statues, family portraits from the skillful brush of Makofski [*sic*], and an extensive conservatory filled with palms, lemon-trees and rare orchids from the tropics. . . . The library, which was another spacious apartment, was filled with well-selected books, newspapers, and magazines, in three or four languages, and contained also a large collection of Siberian minerals and ores.[2]

Anna Nikolaevna's memoirs tell us little about the time she spent back at home, but, after finishing the memoirs, she copied out passages from 1888 to 1889 from the diary that she kept, and these are included here.[3] The diary recounts her older sister's wedding, which many from Nerchinsk Zavod attended. Into this story she weaves the details of a would-be love affair. Providentially she used the diary she kept as a nineteen-year-old girl, so it is particularly fresh and funny.

Finally, the memoirs recount the impact on Anna Nikolaevna of her mother's death. Convinced that she could have saved her mother had she been a doctor, she resolved to overcome her father's opposition and other significant obstacles to attain a medical education in the distant capital of the Russian Empire, St. Petersburg. The chapter concludes with a description of her month-long journey from eastern Siberia to St. Petersburg in 1894, at the age of twenty-four, where she hoped to begin her medical education.

MEMOIRS

The Stages of My Life

I reached the age of seventy-eight in December 1947. Such a long span provides one with the basis for reviewing one's life. The words "stages of my life" remind me of a book I read recently about the Volga–Moscow canal. Just as ships traveling there through the canal rise by stages to the calm heights of the "water bridge" and descend, again by stages, my life flowed in the same way. The different stages of my life gave me the opportunity to rise, in the sense that I developed intellectually and socially. In those days, when it was difficult for women to gain access to higher education, especially for those living in the wilds far from the centers, I was able to achieve the position of doctor, participate in scientific research, carry out cultural and educational work, teach in institutions of higher education, earn the title of professor, and direct the Department of Psychology, and then, narrowing the scale of my work, descend, as it were, by stages to the narrow family role of grandmother.

What was the force that gave me the strength to rise? It was, undoubtedly, the striving for knowledge, an interest in science, and my moral purpose— the desire to be of use to the people. Individuals and literature influenced, developed, and strengthened my strivings, but I acquired my first start in this direction from my family. I begin my memoir with a description of our family.

Our Family and Ancestors

I spent my early childhood, until age seven, at the mine "Gornyi Zerentui." My father was the mine manager and we lived in a government house with five rooms, a garden, and a kitchen garden. There were a number of children. My father, Nikolai Mikhailovich Zhukov, was the son of a blacksmith working in the Kutomarsk silver smelting works. My father's grandfather was a Don Cossack sent to Siberia for his participation in the Pugachev uprising.[4] My father had only a lower education: he finished a village school. An able student, he was sent to the then just-opened lower-level mining school in Nerchinsk Zavod. The administrative center for the mining district was located at that time in Nerchinsk Zavod. Gold prospecting was increasing in the taiga, and mining engineers were in short supply. My father had begun work in the lowest ranks in the mine and had gradually risen higher. When he became forty he attained the rank of mine director.

My mother—Agrafena Afanasevna—was a Savinsky. Her father was a low-level employee in the "Klichka" mine. The mine had closed early on, and the employees were let go. My mother's father, Afanasy Stepanovich, took up farming. The inhabitants of Klichka held him in much respect; they turned to him for various types of advice. His father, Stepan, had been exiled to Siberia for political reasons. While the mine was in operation there had been a prison for political prisoners in Klichka. The Savinskys were friends with several political prisoners. According to my mother's sister's tales, my mother shared a mutual attraction with one of the exiles—Kozlov. Mother was then sixteen years old. He brought Grushenka books to read.[5] Under his influence, Mama took to reading books, and she developed a worldview broader than that of other girls. Before long Kozlov was transferred somewhere.

Mama had a highly attractive appearance. Her gentleness and thoughtfulness gave her a special charm. Father in his old age, when Mama had already died, told us how he married Grushenka. She was his second wife. His parents chose his first wife. When the first wedding took place, the Savinsky sisters came to the evening party from Klichka. Father said: "When I saw Grushenka my heart suddenly began to thump, I didn't understand what the matter was. I was completely stupefied; only later I began to think: 'Here is the one I should have married,' but by then it was too late."

Within a year his wife died in childbirth. He began to court Grushenka. She did not like him. However, owing to the insistence of her father, who had two grown daughters besides her, she had to marry Zhukov. He honored her all his life, and she had a good influence on him. All during her married life, notwithstanding frequent pregnancies and the births of children, she never stopped being crazy about reading books. Father regarded her passion for books indulgently, although the household lacked care because

Fig. 1.1. Anna Zhukova's parents, Agrafena Afanasevna and
Nikolai Mikhailovich Zhukov.

of it. He himself brought her books from the Nerchinsk Zavod library. In
addition, he subscribed to the journal *Niva* with its supplement of novels.[6]
He read little himself but was always interested in technology. When he saw
some new technological developments in the illustrations of *Niva,* he called
us children together and showed it to us, saying with delight, "The mind of
man at work!" He was the first to order a sewing machine. That was a big
event for all the housewives. Before that, they knew only hand sewing. He
bought an expensive clock with a cuckoo and was delighted with the mechanism. Although he had not been educated himself, he strove to provide his
children with education. He didn't begrudge money spent on teachers. He
sent his oldest son, Vanya, to study in Irkutsk.

Father had a large frame: he was tall, broad-shouldered, and strong. He had a stern character. When he was roused to anger, he shouted roughly and was ready to strike the guilty party. An instance of his anger springs to mind. We three girls slept on the floor in the nursery; there was a bed for the nanny, and next to the bed a cradle for our littlest brother. Once when Father came into the children's room, he found it messy; it smelled of diapers, and there were cockroaches next to the stove. He started in accusing Nanny of laziness. She answered him rudely. He went into a fury, stamped his feet, made fists, and raised his arm as if he wanted to strike the old woman. Mama quickly came between them and quieted him down. When they both had left, Nanny told us that she didn't want to live with us any longer, that she was going away, and she began to gather her things into a bundle. She was very querulous, and we watched her preparations without caring. She took her bundle and left the house. From the window we saw this short, fat woman with a big bundle going across the yard and, stopping in the middle, turn, not to the gate but toward our bathhouse in the corner of the yard. Mama heard about Nanny's departure and became worried. Father's sister, who was living with us, calmed her down, saying that Nanny would lie in the bathhouse, cry a little, and come back. But Mama answered, "It would be hard for her to bear the shame, and hard to return uninvited and unbidden." Throwing on a shawl, Mama went to the bathhouse and soon brought Nanny back, helping her to carry her bundle.

For all her gentleness and modesty Mama's moral authority ruled the house. She never used swear words, and no one dared curse in the house. If my older sisters began to ridicule one or another of their acquaintances, she always stopped them with the words: "Rather than judging others, it is better to look to oneself, so that you won't be worse." She didn't allow lies even in jokes. If Father became angry with us children, she always tried to soften his anger; and thanks to that, no one of us in our entire lives ever suffered any physical punishments. The goodness she showed people, her readiness to help the needy, evoked love and respect among those around her.

Many of Father's relatives were poor, and Mama tried to help them all as much as she could; there weren't any poor among the Savinskys. Mama's younger sister often came to our home to visit. We called her Aunt Lyolichka. Her arrival was always a holiday for everyone. She was gay and industrious. We had no hired servants in our house, but Mama always had helpers among Father's relatives. Father's sister, Nadezhda Mikhailovna, frequently lived with us for months at a time. She and her niece on her husband's side ran the kitchen. Nanny was Father's aunt, and there were two nephews, the boys Grisha and Mitya, who studied with the teacher and helped out around the house. All these relatives worked leisurely, almost without Mama's supervision. On her arrival, Lyolichka always saw every kind of fault in the housekeeping and drew everyone into brisk work with her energy. She sewed us dresses, cut our hair and that of others, and good-naturedly reproached

Mama: "You love to read books, but the little children are in a state of ne-glect." Mama didn't like sewing or cooking. She loved to work in the veg-etable garden. As soon as spring came, she forgot her books and worked all day in the garden. Her cucumbers always came up earlier than anyone else's. In the fall she had melons and watermelons growing under glass, some-thing that happened rarely in that climate. My older sisters helped a little, but they were responsible for looking after their younger brothers. With Lyolichka's arrival everyone's spirits rose. She organized spirited games with us and played tricks on the adults. I remember how jokingly she weaned Nanny from conversations about the *domovoi*, the house spirit.[7] After din-ner Nanny recounted how almost every night the *domovoi* smothered her. Pretending to believe Nanny, Lyolichka asked: "What does he look like?"

"It's well known—he's hairy, with horns."

"It can happen that the *domovoi* smothers not for evil but for good," said Lyolichka. "Today, don't eat much in the evening, go to bed early, and when the *domovoi* comes, ask him if he's supporting good or evil."

Nanny carried all this out and actually fell asleep early on her bed. Lyo-lichka let us know beforehand, and we watched what happened with inter-est. A tallow candle standing on a tray on the floor dimly lit our nursery. Lyolichka turned a black fur coat inside out and put it on. She carefully moved the cradle away from the bed and, in her fur, fell upon Nanny. Nanny first rolled over, to get free, then began to mutter: "Do you do evil or good?" We burst out laughing. Lyolichka jumped away, also laughing. Nanny un-derstood what was going on and, abashed, rolled herself up in the blanket right up to her head. In the morning Lyolichka explained to her that it isn't the *domovoi* that smothers her at night but too much food. After that, Nanny never mentioned the *domovoi* again.

The Savinsky family had an educated attitude toward superstition and toward life in general, in spite of their simple peasant lifestyle. Their friend-ship to political exiles influenced them, of course, and [Mama's] grandfa-ther, Stepan Savinsky, exiled on political charges, had some education.

I remember Mama's attitude concerning church ceremonies. Once, when Nanny complained to Mama about her own son, Misha, who didn't want to go to church, Mama answered, "What is he, a monk? Why should he waste his time hanging around a church?"

My father, N. M. Zhukov, grew up in an uneducated environment. He was indifferent to questions of religion, but he observed the traditions of church holidays (attending mass in church, entertaining guests, and drink-ing). In Gugda, the taiga mine where we lived, there was no village or church nearby. On the mornings of big holidays (Easter and Christmas) my father gathered us children together in a room before the icon, and he himself stood in front of us and prayed silently (he crossed himself and kissed the icon) and we had to pray the same way. This lasted no more than five min-utes, and then he took the ladle, previously prepared with incense, and burned it, so that the perfume of incense would be sufficiently dispersed throughout the apartment. After this, we had to approach him in turn and wish him a happy holiday. Mama did not take part in these ceremonies. Father was very hospitable; he always invited guests, and holidays ended with drinking and card games.

Mother had different dreams in life. Life in the big, hastily built government house at the mine oppressed her—its walls without plaster, the floors not painted, comfortless, with mountains and the stumps of the cut-down forest all around. She dreamed of living better in a little *izbushka*[8] surrounded by beautiful nature, for example, on the shores of Lake Baikal. Once, when I was studying there, my father took her to Irkutsk. The sight of Baikal sent her into rapture.

My Childhood and Youth

According to Mother's stories I was born a weakling and wasn't breast-fed since Mother had no milk. I had symptoms of rickets; I began to walk only in my third year, but my speech developed well. When I was four years old my sisters—Sasha, eight years old, and Tanya, nine years old—began to learn to read. When their teacher came to them, I had already taken a position under the table so I could listen to how they learned. After the teacher left, my sisters showed me the alphabet. So I learned to read at the same time as my sisters. Father and Mother were amazed at my success. When guests came, they showed me off. The guests would say some word, and I would choose the necessary letters from cut-out letters scattered on the floor and form the given word. Later I openly studied with my sisters as an equal. Our studies went without any particular system, and our teachers often changed. When I was eleven, my sisters learned that there was a high school in Irkutsk, with a boarding department for children of state employees, and they began to beg Father to send me to Irkutsk. Father did not agree at first. I myself gave it little thought. I remember one moment when my sisters convinced me to ask Father myself. Father was strict with us, and we were timid about approaching him. At my sisters' instigation, I decided to go to his office, where Father lay on the couch. Crossing the threshold, I said quickly from the doorway, "Papa, send me to Irkutsk to study!" and immediately ran away. Whether it was my request or something else that influenced him, Father did decide to send me to Irkutsk in the fall.

Reminiscences of Life at the Gugda Mine in the Taiga

Our father, N. M. Zhukov, despite the fact that he did not have even a high school education, was assigned more than once to run newly opened gold fields in the taiga.[9] Mining engineers did not want to go off to the taiga, and the administration unwillingly named practical workers such as our father as managers. At first he managed the Bulatka mine, and then he was transferred to Gugda. That was in 1880. In our family there were seven children at that time. My oldest brother, Vanya, studied in Irkutsk and came home only for the summer. My sisters, Tanya, fifteen, and Sasha, fourteen, were older than I. I was eleven. The youngest were my brothers Kesha, five, Afonya, four, and the newborn, Misha. The house for the manager in Gugda looked hastily built; its log walls were neither plastered nor whitewashed, and the floors in its five big rooms were unpainted.

Mama was unhappy in this big, uncomfortable house, and said, "It would be better to live in a little bit of a house on the shores of Baikal; here there is nothing to see except mountains and stumps."

The forest was cut down around the mine, and there were more stumps visible on the hills than trees. On the hill opposite our house, Father allowed us girls to build bonfires around the stumps to burn them up. We cleaned a place around each stump so that the fire wouldn't spread, brought dry twigs to the stump and lit them. Late in the evening, when it was getting dark, we feasted our eyes on the fires on the mountain, as if it were an illumination.

Another distraction for us was to watch the progress of the work of extracting gold. There were many workers at the mine, and there were horses with two-wheeled carriages. Work was always in full swing on the big square between the mountains. The laborers worked by hand; they removed the peat [*torf*] with pick and shovel, making what was called a "cut" of a depth not less than a *sazhen*.[10] The peat that was removed was loaded onto a carriage and thrown on the dump. And so it went until they reached the gold-bearing rock. The "machine" stood in the middle of the cut. That's what the wooden structure with three tiers was called. On the top was the platform, enclosed by a railing, and in the middle of the platform was the hole where they poured the rock. The workers led the horse with the loaded carriage by the reins up the planking that led to the platform, raised the rock, and poured it from the carriage into the hole. Falling below, the rock fell on an iron grate where iron "shoes," rotating on a wheel, pulverized it. Two pairs of horses below turned the wheel. Only small rocks fell down through small holes in the grate; the stones were thrown into a special container that opened at the bottom and were taken to the dump. The rock that went through the opening fell on a sloping, graded plane with depressions, into which water from a channel flowed. The water carried the light parts of rock away, and the sand with gold stuck in the depressions. At the end of the working day two trustworthy specialists from among the workers came to wash the gold. This took place solemnly, under the supervision of the employees and the manager himself. The gold extracted was carried to the office under lock and seal.

The washing of the gold depended on the availability of water. In Gugda water for the machine flowed from a stream along a wooden channel. When there was a summer with a long drought, the stream grew shallow, water didn't flow in the channel, and the washing of gold ceased. For the manager, who was obliged to carry out strict orders on the amount of gold extracted, droughts were a complete catastrophe. I quote a note from my childhood journal, where I described from memory how we lived through a drought in Gugda:

> I remember how for a month one summer there wasn't a drop of rain. The sultry air was heavy with "heat haze" [*marevo*], that is, with a kind of heavy exhalation mixed with the smoke from forest fires. This "heat haze" produced a murky curtain through which the sun was visible like a red lamp. It was difficult to breathe and miserable even for us children. Father was gloomy. He walked back and forth on the terrace, angrily, hopelessly looking at the cloudless horizon. There was hope only in God. Father twice sent horses to the nearest village for a priest to conduct a service, but, on various pretexts, the priest refused to come. Finally, we heard from someone that the priest could come. Father sent horses immediately. A young, tall priest came and with him a rascally, fat sexton. They brought all the equipment for a prayer service. Father arranged that all the workers and employees gathered for the service. A table, covered with a white cloth, was placed in the "cut," not far from the machine. During the service the priest sang repeatedly in a high tenor, "Give rain to the suffering earth, Savior!" The sexton echoed him in a hoarse bass. Many of those gathered diligently crossed themselves and fell on their knees, probably believing sincerely that, after their prayer, God would send rain and coolness. In the crowd of workers, those indifferent [to prayer] stood out, unmoving. In choosing the day for the prayer service the priest made no mistake in his calculating; obviously he guided himself by the barometer's indication of rain. That very day, toward the evening, clouds appeared on the horizon, and the next day came pouring rain. Water flowed to the machine and work began again.
>
> In this way, then, naively, the question of battling with drought was settled.

The workers in the gold fields were peasants from nearby villages, prisoners released from prison, and simply vagrants. They worked from 6:00 in the morning to 6:00 in the evening, without any holiday breaks. There were only two days off a month—every first and fifteenth day of the month. On those days, the workers received "a ration," that is, a glass of raw spirits mixed with water. This took place usually on our terrace. Two workers brought a tub of spirits on a pole. The repulsive smell of unpurified spirits spread over the whole terrace. The workers were called from a list, in alphabetical order. Among them were many Ivans Without-a-family or Ivans I-don't-remember; they were called by number—the first Ivan I-don't-remember, the second, and so on.[11] We also ran into unusual family names. For instance, I remember that someone had the name "Where the sun goes, I go" [*Kuda solntse, tuda i ia*]. That is what he was called in order to receive the "ration." Each worker tossed off his glass of spirits and gasped with pleasure.

There weren't any cultural diversions for the workers nor even any mention of any. Not content with their "ration," workers bought vodka from secret alcohol traders, and all day drunken songs resounded, cursing was heard, and fights frequently broke out. Workers were housed in barracks where they slept side by side on bunks. Those with families lived in tiny little huts. Each worker received a book when he was hired, which held records of the provisions and clothes the worker was given. In the fall the cost of what the worker had received was subtracted from his earnings, and so the worker ended up with very little in his hands and some had nothing left. So as not to leave penniless, they unwillingly accepted work for the following summer and received an advance. Many workers drank up the money they had received as soon as they reached the next village down the road—Kultum—where a merchant had earlier prepared the bait, laying vodka, various expensive wines, and so forth, in stock. And there were workers who "pilfered" at the mine, that is, secretly washed gold in the chutes, and they had a lot of money and gold. Among these workers one met men who liked to do things in a big way. It was said that in Kultum they gave full scope to their debauchery: they bought red calico by the whole piece and laid it out like a rug; they caroused along the streets of the village with young girls to the music of the harmonica; they drank champagne and snacked on herring and *omul'*;[12] they rented a troika of horses for riding; and so on. After such debauchery, having spent all their capital, some returned to the mine to get an advance on future work. If peasants who had received an advance did not appear on the mine in the spring, they were forced to return by the police.

There were even instances of murder at the mine. I remember how once the mine inhabitants were upset by the murder of the worker Barkhatov. He was well known as a young, strong man, a dandy, and handsome in the gypsy fashion. Many, including us girls, went to look at the victim out of curiosity. I can still remember the great impression it made on me. In a clearing surrounded by little shrubs the murder victim lay in his elegant rose-colored shirt, in wide, black velveteen trousers. The powerful man was motionless, his face to the ground, and the rose-colored shirt fluttered in a little breeze. People said that jealousy was the motive for the murder. A worker's life was valued little then, and there was no investigation of the murder.

In the fall, when work ended and workers dispersed homeward, life at the mine became more peaceful; it emptied out and became quiet. The dogs howled at night, smelling the approach of wolves, and, on leaving the house, one could hear wolves howling in the forest. Workers who were staying through the winter sat in their houses without any kind of social amusements. I spent only one winter at the mine; the following fall Father took me away to study in Irkutsk, and I only came home to Gugda during the summer holidays.

What sheer holidays these homecomings were for me. Our family was affectionate. Everyone tried to do something nice for me, as a dear guest, especially my sisters. Tanya had already completely freed Mama from house-work, and she tried to offer me everything she considered a delicacy. Both of them tried to dress me up more beautifully, and I delighted in walks in the woods, games with my little brothers, and the closeness of all my be-loved family.

School in Irkutsk

That year [1882] Father was manager of the Gugda mine.[13] We children lived freely. We ran far into the woods, not fearing wolves, gathered berries, and in a little river went fishing for little fish with our kerchiefs. We loved to burn dry grass in the forest glades, taking care not to burn the trees. My departure for Irkutsk cut short my carefree life. The high school with the boarding department was called "The Institute for Noble Girls." In the beginning it was interesting to live in a three-story stone house. But soon I felt the weight of the strict regime of the monotonous days. Each step was under the super-vision of the classroom mistress [*klassnaia dama*]. We could stroll only in the courtyard, in pairs, with calm steps—running and jumping were forbidden. Looking out the window, I thought, "Even the prisoners in the mines live better; they are taken to the mountains where they work."

I was homesick. This was combined with the unpleasant sensation of not getting enough to eat. In the morning one glass of tea with a small white roll. For the second breakfast between classes, they brought a tray with slices of black bread. Each girl was given one slice of bread that she had to eat in the corridor before the beginning of class. Eating coarse, often poorly baked bread without any kind of liquid was unpleasant. Many girls were devious and hid their slice in their pockets so that later, quietly, out of sight of the classroom mistress, they could dry it in the oven. The dried bread seemed to taste better.

The three-course dinner on holidays was more substantial. For supper there was inevitable *forshmak*—potato mixed with herring. In our dormi-tory, next to me, was Anichka Kozlova's bed; at night we dreamed of run-ning away from the institute and discussed our plan of escape, although we were conscious of the futility of the plan, since her home was as far from Irkutsk as mine.

The institute had the program of a high school (gymnasium) with two preparatory classes for those with less formal education. In the preparatory classes we began to study French and German right away. I did not know any foreign languages; nonetheless I was assigned to the first class, and I had a very difficult time making up for my insufficient knowledge. I remember how I copied from one of the students the words I didn't understand in the German lesson. Tears ran down my face onto my notebook and made blots.

The teacher showed my notebook to the whole class later, brandishing the dirtiest page with indignation. The girls tittered, and I suffered deeply. In the course of a year I caught up with the class in knowledge of foreign languages.

From the second year on, I was already the top student and continued to be the best for the remaining six years of study. I took up drawing with a special passion; if there was any time free from lessons, I went to the art room and copied plaster figures from life. The monotonous life in the institute for "noble girls" was saturated with church rituals: we had to attend church services. The church was on the third floor, where we had our sleeping room, our dormitory. Women on duty read prayers aloud in the morning and before we lay down to sleep, before each meal and after we ate. During exams we were led into the empty church, where we had to kiss the icon and pray that we would pass each exam. Every other kind of superstition also existed; we were afraid of ghosts and we believed that the portrait of the empress left its frame at night and that the dead empress walked along the corridors. The sleeping rooms and corridors were dimly lit from above by kerosene lamps (there were no electric lamps then).

Before bedtime, when the girls were still roaming about the corridors, it took only some hysterical girl to cry wildly, "Ai! She's walking!" for all to fling themselves madly down the stairs. The girls of the older classes, in spite of strict supervision, contrived to carry on romantic correspondence with military school cadets. During their walks in the courtyard they used to throw little notes over the fence and receive notes from them through agreed-on slits in the fence.

A new school inspector, Konstantin Frantsevich Lukashevich, brought a lively spirit into the stagnant atmosphere of our life.[14] He began by improving the material conditions: at his insistence they increased our portions of white bread at breakfast, and, at the second breakfast, instead of a slice of black bread, they began to give us a hot, substantial meal. Walks in the courtyard became free, and we could walk in the streets in pairs and along the banks of the Angara. At that time there was an earthen parapet along the Angara bank, where people of Irkutsk strolled on holidays. We particularly valued Konstantin Frantsevich's friendly attitude to us: he joined us without ceremony in our free time; we surrounded him in a close circle and went down the halls, listening to him talk about subjects that we didn't usually hear about. There were tales of famous scholars, new developments in science, and such. One could see in all these conversations what sort of life he might consider good, how one should live so as to be useful to the people, to one's country. He was able to say all this sincerely with genuine concern for our future. Conversations with him broadened our horizons; they led us out of the narrow world of our institutional education, where all that was demanded was that we could curtsey well, speak French, and so on.

We were only allowed to read proper children's books. Literary classics— Dostoevsky, Turgenev—were forbidden. In the higher classes I made friends with Asya Tagunova whose brother, Yasha, visited on Sundays. He had been expelled from the university because of political "unreliability." He brought, [hidden] in a basket under cookies of various kinds, the forbidden books of Dostoevsky, Turgenev, and others. Asya furtively hid the book she got under her bedding. At night, when everyone was asleep and the classroom mistress had gone to her own room, Asya and I quietly got up and, half-dressed, set out through the dark corridors to the little music room. I was studying music and had received a piece of stearin candle so that I could prepare my lessons. I saved the candle ends, and Asya and I, settling down in a little corner behind the piano, read Dostoevsky's *Brothers Karamazov* and *The Idiot*, *On The Eve* by Turgenev, and other books. Thus life, apart from that in official channels, percolated down to us.

Some actions of the administration also pushed us toward critical thinking. For example, before the appearance of Konstantin Frantsevich, when I was in the second year, the best student, Dusya Olizarenko, was expelled from the third class. She was expelled simply because her father was a gardener. Only the daughters of white-collar employees and merchants could study in the institute for "noble girls." We were very sorry for this sweet girl. Subsequently we recalled that if we had had Konstantin Frantsevich with us then, he would not have allowed such an unjust expulsion.

When I was in the last year, not long before graduation, some sort of important inspector came to us from Petersburg. Apparently, to get us to show how we were thinking, he gave us this theme for a classroom essay: "Which book I liked the best, and why?" Lyusya Tagunova, Asya's sister, had the carelessness to write that she liked Turgenev's book, *Fathers and Sons*, best of all.[15] A big scandal erupted. The inspector blamed the administration. After stormy discussions, it was decided to deny Lyusya the certificate showing that she had finished the course. Only the intercession of her father, who had some kind of important post in the police, preserved her right to the certificate.

I will use a section from my childhood diary to describe how graduation went:

15 May 1888. Exams are finished. I was nominated for the highest prize—a large-sized gold medal [*shifr*]. The graduation ceremony will be in three days and then: farewell institutional life! Joy and terror! What lies ahead for me? Konstantin Frantsevich spoke correctly, that we do not know life and are not ready for it. I was often miserable inside the official institute walls and now am sorry that I have to leave.

18 May 1888. Today was graduation. Everything was very festive. The Count and Countess Ignatev attended with two adjutants, and many other guests. After prayer and the inspector's and the headmistress's speeches we were called alphabetically to receive our certificates. When my turn came, and I walked to the middle of the hall, Konstantin Frantsevich suddenly stopped me and began a laudatory speech. He began by saying that the highest

award—the medal—did not adequately describe my personality; he said that I always, on my own initiative, helped the weak students, that the whole class prepared for exams with my help, and some other things. I was in no state to listen; blood was rushing to my head. My ears were ringing, it seemed to me that I was rooted to the ground in the middle of the hall, I wished I could shrink, I didn't know what to do with my hands. When Konstantin Frantsevich finally finished, and I, having gotten my certificate, walked back, I met the mocking look of the adjutant. When I came even with him, he said ironically, "Well, how will you justify in your life all that Konstantin Frantsevich said about you." I blushed further and did not answer. At the end of graduation the Countess Ignateva gave a speech. In her speech she spoke ill of the Higher Women's Courses that existed then in Petersburg, saying the courses led to atheism, to diverse evil thoughts, and warned that if any of us took it into her head to attend these courses, she would discredit the institution![16]

Before that no one had spoken to us of the possibility of higher education for women. The countess's speech made no impression on me. Under the influence of conversations with Konstantin Frantsevich I felt an obligation after the institute to live an industrious life and to be of use to people. Thinking thus, it seemed to me that being a teacher was a useful activity.

Return to Nerchinsk Zavod

However, the fact of the matter was that, after returning home, for the first two years I lived the ordinary life of a gentry miss of that time: I went to dance evenings, took part in amateur performances, and so on. In the first year I fell for the teacher, Ivan Ivanovich Orlov, who brought me books to read while courting me, spoke beautifully on lofty themes, and seemed to me to be an ideal person. I even dreamed that I would marry him; together we would work in a school, devise better methods of teaching, and so on. Disillusionment came fairly quickly. It began in a small way: we were sitting once at the dinner table when a guest told a stupid, dirty joke. Ivan Ivanovich suddenly burst out with suppressed laughter and sprang up from the table. I was astonished. Soon, a good friend of ours came from Nerchinsk Zavod. Ivan Ivanovich was renting a room from her. In conversation with Mama, in front of me, she told stories describing him as a debauched fellow. I was sick to hear it. I endured my grief at night, in tears, and my infatuation disappeared. Somehow I made him understand, and he stopped coming to see us.

Youth
Pages kept from the youthful diary of Anna Zhukova.
(Copied, keeping the former orthography)[17]

May 30th, 1888. Tonya Ryndina and I are going home from Irkutsk, on post horses. The next to the last post station is Solontsa. It's a little station

Fig. 1.2. Anna Zhukova, age unknown (probably about eighteen years old).

surrounded by forest. It turned out we spent the night here; in the morning we both woke early with the thought that today, toward evening, we would be home. We leapt up gaily, having slept without changing clothes, and rushed out on the street. The sun hadn't yet risen. What a fabulous morning! Sweet cool air comes from the forest; from afar a cuckoo bird is coo-cooing and somewhere nearby little bells are calling. It's easy to breathe. Tonya and I clasp hands and we want to fly in the clear air, in the rosy light of morning dawn, soar high and embrace the whole world. It's good, it's wonderfully good to be alive! . . . Soon, soon we'll be home!

September 5th. I haven't written for more than three months. It's great to be home. But I'm not at peace with myself: all I do is eat, sleep, walk about; there's not even anything to read but the supplement to *Niva*. Konstantin Frantsevich's words about shameful, idle lives come back to me, how one should work for the good of the people. But what am I to do?

Masha Pastukhova—she's a complete orphan, and can work right away as a public schoolteacher, but Father won't let me go away. One of the [mine] employees asked me to teach his two little girls to read. I agreed gladly. I spend time with my little brother, Kolya. He's three years old. I'm not the only one, everyone loves him.

On St. Peter's Day[18] the teacher Ivan Ivanovich Orlov came from Nerchinsk Zavod to see us (at the Lopatikha mine). He was my friend Nadya's husband. Two months after the wedding she died of smallpox. He is tall, a handsome brunette with shining gray eyes and he can look right into your soul with them. For some reason or other, the very first day he came, when we were standing together on the terrace, he asked permission to call me simply Anna. I was embarrassed, I didn't know what to say and silently nodded my head.[19] There's something special about him. While he was at our house, it was gay and lively. In conversation with him I felt like a complete ignoramus. I have to read more. He promised to send me Byron and Shakespeare. I don't know them at all. It's a shame Ivan Ivanovich could stay only two days with us. He was very attentive to me the whole time: he frequently repeated my words as though he attached special value to them. After his departure, life fell back into its routine.

October 4th. Now winter is approaching. Work in the mine has finished and the majority of the workers have dispersed. The mine has taken on a sad look and it's not gay at home. The preparations for my sister Sashenka's wedding are the only thing of interest. Her dowry is being sewn. My elder sister, Tanichka, bustles about more than anyone: all the domestic preparations for celebrating the wedding and the dowry preparations lie on her shoulders. Sashenka is busy with the delicate, fine work. I'm given the less responsible work such as stitching the loops on the pillowcases, and so on. Once a week the postman comes from Nerchinsk Zavod with the mail—the newspaper *The Eastern Review* comes from Irkutsk and one issue of *Niva*. Sometimes I get a letter and books from Ivan Ivanovich. His letters are always interesting and make me want to answer them right away; but my letter will lie about for a week till the next post.

November 12th. Sashenka's wedding took place. Our house was full of guests who came from Nerchinsk Zavod (thirty versts away).[20] Ivan Ivanovich came and the engineer Lovitsky, whom the mine gossips consider Tanichka's fiancé. Sashenka told me in secret that Tanya is in love with Lovitsky. We were expecting our favorite aunt, Lyolichka (Mama's sister), but only Aunt Nadezhda Mikhailovna (Papa's sister) came. At the beginning the girls and women danced to the music of fiddlers, the Belovinsky brothers, brought in from Nerchinsk Zavod.[21] I wore a pale blue dress that had been made for me in Irkutsk for graduation. I'm told it becomes me. I am a blonde after Father, my hair curls slightly; my summer sunburn is gone from my face; my cheeks are rosy.[22] Engineer Lovitsky courted me obviously which was awkward for me in front of Tanichka. I wasn't pleased that Lovitsky asked

me straightaway for all the quadrilles, but I couldn't refuse. He seems unin-
teresting to me in comparison with Ivan Ivanovich; he carries on conversations that are somehow always trite, although on the exterior he is imposing.
I danced a lot of light dances with Ivan Ivanovich. He loves to waltz and
dances with enthusiasm. Apparently he was not pleased with the engineer's
attentions to me: the next day after breakfast he expressed his annoyance
in front of everybody but in such a way that it was clear to me alone. He can
talk that way. That day we went to the village of Duchary, eight versts away,
for Sashenka's wedding ceremony. Tanya went with the bride and groom;
and I went in the same sled with Ivan Ivanovich and Auntie Nadezhda Mikhailovna. The whole road was studded with troikas, bells rang and little
bells jingled; and there were many-colored ribbons draped on the horses'
manes. The day was brilliantly sunny. The fat mine horses whirled us gaily
on the even road. Ivan Ivanovich protected me from the snow spray the
lead horse kicked up in my face. We laughed a lot. I don't laugh a lot in
general, but Ivan Ivanovich is witty and can make one laugh.

The little village church was filled up with our wedding train and local
curiosity seekers. I began to feel sad in the church. Sashenka, striking in
her elegant white dress, with a magnificent bridal veil on her head, stood
beneath the crown;[23] but suppressed grief was reflected in her face. Her
look of suffering made her look like a holy martyr. Her fiancé, in his officer's
uniform, stood triumphant, with an unpleasantly self-satisfied look on his
face. Sashenka is marrying without love. When Mikhail Kuzmich Okuntsov
proposed to her, she refused him. He began to importune her persistently
and threatened to shoot himself. Sashenka is too sweet. The thought of
being the cause of someone's death terrified her, and she reluctantly agreed
to marry him. She liked the teacher Bunkov, but he rarely came to see us.
Before the wedding, in order to calm Mama and us down, she began saying
that now she likes Mikhail Kuzmich, but we didn't believe her as we didn't
like him ourselves. In church the tears I held back choked me. I was afraid
that I would burst out crying, which would have been inappropriate during
a wedding.

I went back home with Ivan Ivanovich again. After the stuffiness of the
church it was pleasant to breathe the fresh, slightly frosty air. It was good to
sit down, and I would have liked to ride on and on. We didn't laugh on the
road but had a friendly, serious conversation. It was too bad that we soon
got home.

14 XI [November]. Yesterday we escorted Sashenka and her husband.
How she sobbed, saying good-bye to us and especially to Mama. Mommy
completely fell apart. Tanya and I cried a long time at night, and in the
morning when we woke up were frightened by our looks; we both had puffy
eyelids and swollen noses. We had to put cold compresses on for a long
time before leaving our room. Our guests had not yet all dispersed. Engineer Lovitsky had gone, but Ivan Ivanovich stayed for about three more

days. In the evening we played post office. How beautifully Ivan Ivanovich can express so much in so few words. . . . I can't understand why Tanya doesn't like him.

15 XI. Today, at dinner, this happened. Auntie's husband, Mitrofan Maksimovich, whom we don't like because of his laziness and disreputable nature, told some kind of stupid and dirty joke. It was unpleasant for everybody, but Ivan Ivanovich suddenly burst out laughing and fled from the table to another room. This amazed me. Is it possible that he liked such filthy things? This reminded me that Tanya had heard somewhere that on his writing table there is a pornographic statuette. I didn't believe it then.

16 XI. Today Ivan Ivanovich read aloud Nekrasov's "Knight for an Hour."[24] How sincere, how heartfelt his voice sounded! I was ashamed that I thought badly of him yesterday. There is absolutely nothing common about him. You feel that he himself is a knight, not just for an hour but for his whole life. Yes, surely he will do something great in life, something pure, and will not drag his life out among "idle chatterers." Recently I read a novel by Sheller-Mikhailov.[25] In it one couple's happy life is described. He and she teach in a public school, they have common aspirations and ideals. They have lots of troubles; but together they bear everything steadfastly and love each other with a sublime love.

16 XI. Ivan Ivanovich has left. How dark and deserted everything in the house is without him! I listen involuntarily, won't his steps resound, won't his voice be heard . . . in spite of the fact that I know he isn't here. What a profound and sad look he had when he said good-bye. He gave me his photograph in remembrance. How wonderful it is that he had it with him. I wrapped it in a pink cigarette paper and put it in the front corner of the drawer in the writing table so that I could open and look at it without Tanya noticing. I can't understand why Tanya so doesn't like Ivan Ivanovich. He has such a noble soul! And when I unwrap the pink paper to look at the picture it seems to me that his whole face shines, indeed beams radiate from it. What is he doing now? Tanya is going to Nerchinsk Zavod to do errands tomorrow. She's lucky! She might see Ivan Ivanovich.

21 XI 88. Tanya has finally arrived. I was so looking forward to her arrival. Our acquaintance, Agrafinya Filimonovna, from whom Ivan Ivanovich rents a room, came with her. I hesitated to ask Tanya whether she had seen Ivan Ivanovich, but in the evening she was reciting miscellaneous news to Auntie. She purposely raised her voice, saying that at the Lukins' she had met Ivan Ivanovich and saw he is courting Lida Lukina in earnest, that it is clear he wants to propose to her. I wanted to cry out, "It's not true!" but I held back. Though I know that Tanya can't lie; it just seemed that way to her, and she is exaggerating in order to spoil my attitude toward Ivan Ivanovich. Auntie began to argue that Lida is a good match for Orlov, that she is pretty and will be given a rich dowry. There is confusion in my head and a heavy lump lay on my heart. Is it possible?

<u>22 XI</u>. Another blow and this time it was final. I heard a conversation between Agrafinya Filimonovna and Mama. In a calm voice she told Mama that Ivan Ivanovich is counting on marrying the wealthy Lida—indeed, her father is a well-known millionaire; but Agrafinya Filimonovna thinks that her parents won't give Lida in marriage to Ivan Ivanovich, indeed they know about his debauched behavior. Recently in the club the maid Dasha was fired because she was in a certain way. And who is the guilty one? The world teems with rumor; "and how should I not know? After all, Ivan Ivanovich lives in my house." I was in no condition to hear more. Something indeed broke in my breast. I went off to our room; Tanya wasn't there. I opened the desk drawer and unwrapped the picture. A face looked out at me, completely ordinary, no beams radiated from it anymore. I hurled the picture in the back corner of the drawer; let it lie there among useless papers. I lay down on the bed with my face to the wall and, claiming a headache, remained that way till evening.

<u>27 XI</u>. The post came today from Nerchinsk Zavod with a letter for me from Ivan Ivanovich. I opened it without any kind of quiver. More beautiful phrases and allusions to some kind of deep feeling. It's all false! Of course I'm not going to answer. I tore the letter into tiny scraps and threw them into the stove.

<u>January 7, 1889</u>. I haven't written for a long time; there was emptiness in my heart. Tonya Ryndina and Lida Lukina came to visit us for Christmastide. I love Tonya a lot but haven't talked much with Lida; but we became friends over these days. The time with them passed cheerfully, we told fortunes a lot and played various games. On the eve of their departure we didn't go to sleep for a long time: we told each other all our secrets in heart-to-heart conversations. And how funny it was! It turns out that Ivan Ivanovich strenuously courted both Tonya and Lida and did everything as he had with me. Tonya has a sober, observant mind. She told how in the beginning she, too, had been in love and then quickly had become disillusioned with him. We laughed till we cried when Tonya described vividly all Ivan Ivanovich's techniques: in the beginning the long looks, the repetition of words you'd spoken as if they had special worth for him, then allusions to his feelings in front of outsiders but in such words that they would be understandable to one alone, the declamation of poetry, and, in departure, tragic looks and poses. With each of us he had played a role as if he had notes. He is a virtuoso, and we dummies saw an ideal person in him, a profound nature.

Now Tonya loves the forester Serebrennikov, she finds that he has a knight's soul. And what if all of a sudden it turns out that she is mistaken? This thought came to my mind: why do we seek heroism, knightliness in men, and not think about ourselves. Don't we ourselves belong to the "idle chatterers"? Indeed, we don't aspire to anything, we worry only about ourselves and not about the good of the people. The conversations with Konstantin Frantsevich about what sort of life should be considered a good one sprang to my mind.

Preparing for Medical School[26]

Shortly afterward Mama fell very ill. Her illness lasted eight months. At first, we thought she had malaria. We sent the horses many times for the doctor from Nerchinsk Zavod (thirty versts away). A young doctor came, prescribed quinine and went away again, and the patient got worse. Later, it turned out that Mama's blood was infected from carrying a dead fetus. Energetic measures were necessary, and the young doctor continued to prescribe quinine in ever higher doses with each trip. There was no other doctor nearby. So Mama died. It was at that time I got the idea that—if I myself had been a doctor—I could have saved Mama.

My sisters, Tanya and Sasha, were married, and I alone stayed with Father. I had my two younger brothers under my supervision: Misha, nine years old, and Kolya, four years old. Kesha and Afonya were studying in the gymnasium in Chita and lived with our aunt, Demidova.

Soon Father retired. He bought a house on the edge of Nerchinsk Zavod, and we left the mine and went there. In Nerchinsk Zavod there had once been a silver smelting works [*zavod*], but it had long ago been liquidated, and only the name remained. When we moved there, Nerchinsk Zavod was the center for the administration of all the fields and pits of the mining district. There was, besides an elementary school, a mining school, a hospital, a large bazaar square, and a club. The chief of the mining district lived there, as well as mining engineers and rich merchants in large, two-story houses. Shortly after we moved, many parents came to me with requests that I teach their children, and I opened a private school. Twenty-three pupils gathered, the majority girls with only three boys. I divided them into three groups according to their knowledge and invited as helpers two girl-friends who had finished the Irkutsk institute a year later than I.

Father subscribed to Irkutsk and Petersburg newspapers and the journal *Niva* and its supplements. In order not to forget foreign languages I subscribed to a French journal and a German one and read them, occasionally having to resort to dictionaries. From the Petersburg newspaper I found out that a privately funded committee had formed to collect money to open a Women's Medical Institute.[27] They had gotten permission from the tsar and had already begun to build the building. This inspired me; I wanted to slide the walls apart and fly away there. A later report said that to enter the Medical Institute you would need a classical education, that is, knowledge of Latin and Greek. That did not frighten me. I obtained textbooks and tried to understand them on my own. At that time I received a telegram from my elder brother, Vanya, that his wife had fallen very ill, and he asked me to come to him. My brother was serving as an officer in Kara, two hundred versts from Nerchinsk Zavod. Great distances do not frighten Siberians, and I quickly went to Kara, taking my textbooks with me. Lyuba, my brother's wife, earlier had had signs of consumption. That year after the

Fig. 1.3. Children and teachers at the school in Nerchinsk Zavod organized by
Anna Zhukova with her friends, around 1890. She is standing in the last row,
first on the left.

birth of her third child the illness sharply intensified. On my arrival I found
Lyuba so weak that she could not get up from bed. In addition to the six-
month-old baby, they had a three-year-old daughter and a son five years
old. The children were unsupervised, which is what made my brother tele-
graph me. Lyuba suffered from headaches, which in the end became tuber-
cular meningitis. She was in serious condition for more than a month, and
then she died. At the patient's bedside, as at the time when Mama was ill, I
suffered from my helplessness in the face of my lack of medical knowledge.
There was no doctor in Kara. Only a physician's assistant [*feldsher*] visited
the patient. My brother knew my dream and the necessity of studying classical languages. He invited a teacher for me, a political convict. There was a
prison for political convicts in Kara. Those who had already served their
time in prison were considered settlers and could work freely. Such was my
teacher, Fomichev. He came to work with me every other day. I snatched
time during the day by the half hour or hour. At night the baby, who was
bottle-fed, was often restless. Rocking him to sleep in my arms, I opened
one or another textbook and dinned the lesson in. These studies distracted
me from the harsh reality and relieved my life.

My father's sister, Nadezhda Mikhailovna, came soon after Lyuba's burial and replaced me in the care of the children. I went back to Nerchinsk Zavod.

Father opposed my wish to go to Petersburg to study medicine. He knew that the engineer Lovitsky was courting me and thought that this was a great match for me. I myself felt that I had nothing in common with this engineer in views or goals. I didn't even want to get into a conversation with him, and I avoided him in every way possible. I begged Father persistently. I remember once even falling before him on my knees, but he was implacable. My mother's brother, Alexander Afanasevich Savinsky, gave me active support. He had a lot of authority with Father and succeeded in convincing him to agree to let me go and to give me the money to study.

Having won Father's consent, I began to busy myself studying Latin and Greek with even greater fervor. I found a teacher in the political convict Freifeld, who had served out his hard labor in Akatui Prison. He still had ties with the prisoners in Akatui. Peter Yakubovich, whose literary pseudonym was "Melshin," was there at that time. Through Freifeld I received Yakubovich's request to carry the manuscript for his story "From the World of Outcasts" to Petersburg and give it to his brother, Professor V. Yakubovich, together with a letter and portrait of Melshin that a fellow prisoner had drawn. The manuscript and portrait were enclosed in a bulky wooden case. In appealing to me, Yakubovich told me that his brother as a professor would show me every kind of assistance in entering the Medical Institute.[28]

I left Nerchinsk Zavod in August 1894. Father took me to the village of Tontoi, from where I was supposed to travel with a relative, Ivan Kuzmich Okuntsov. He was going to Kazan to enter a theological academy. We had to go across Siberia to Tomsk on horseback, then from Tomsk to Tyumen by steamboat, from Tyumen by railroad to Syzran, from Syzran on steamboat to Nizhny Novgorod, and from there to Petersburg again by railroad.[29] In Kazan Ivan Kuzmich disembarked from the steamboat, and I went on with no fellow travelers. The trip took me thirty-one days. We figured that I arrived quickly, for even the post from Petersburg to Nerchinsk Zavod took no less than thirty-two days. Ivan Kuzmich and I were hurrying to make the beginning of classes. If we found a change of post horses ready at a station we asked them to harness them quickly and rode on, often not even managing to eat. We suffered great chagrin when those traveling for state business outstripped us and took the waiting postal horses; then we had to sit many hours at the station. An unexpected obstacle worked to our benefit. After a pouring rainstorm, the river Zima ran high. On its far side was the station of the same name. The ferry had been swept away; crossing was impossible. The sight of the river dismayed us. Turbid with foam, the water overflowed its banks here and there; in the middle, the rapid current carried bits of wood, sticks, and even a whole tree floated by, torn up by its roots. It was obvious that there was a great delay in the offing. Passengers gathered on the shore, together with women and children from the homes located on the near side of the river. Suddenly we heard loud voices: four tipsy peasants went along the riverbank and cried out, "Who wants to go for a little spin in a boat? We'll bring you quickly to the other side." No one answered. Ivan Kuzmich and I quickly exchanged a few words and decided to risk it. When I went to sit down in the boat, one of the women put her hand on my shoulder and tenderheartedly said: "You're not afraid! You must not have a mother of your own [anymore]." The oarsmen rowed the boat upstream against the current for a long time so as to be able to go past the rocks on the shore of an islet; one had to be able to compute correctly so as to properly include the speed of the current. It was terrifying when the oarsmen argued and then agreed with the one who argued that they would manage to slip past the rocks. Indeed, they managed. Thus outstripping those riders on state business, we arrived quickly at Krasnoyarsk. For the sake of speed we decided to continue by the "old-boys' network." That is what one called the private coachmen who took passengers not to the postal station but to their coachmen friends. They didn't provide a troika with a closed postal carriage but rather a pair of horses with a little cart, on which we fit our meager baggage with difficulty. One time at night we tipped over on some sort of a slope. I was always worried that I might lose the box with Melshin's manuscript. Once, in our hurry, we forgot it in a coachman's hut, under the bench. Having gone part of the way I suddenly remembered it. As a result I had to ask the coachman to go back, for a special fee. Further on there were no particular delays. In Tyumen I saw my first train. Boarding was at night. When we entered the car we saw that sleeping people occupied all the places. The only free seat was by the door. I was delighted that I could travel sitting up, as though in a chair. The transfer to the steamship was not particularly notable: we went third class, on the deck, sitting on our things. The last stage before Petersburg from Nizhny I went in a compartment with a few women. Among them was a young, very sociable woman.

My First Arrival in Petersburg

This woman got everyone involved in general conversation. She told us that she was a ballerina at the Mariinsky Theater. She had fallen ill with a nervous disease and spent the summer in treatment at a sanatorium in the Urals. This was her eighth day on the road. When I said that I had been traveling thirty-one days everyone oohed and ahhed and bombarded me with questions. Finding out that I didn't have acquaintances in Petersburg, the ballerina convinced me to stay with her landlady. For some reason or other I mistrusted her suggestion and said that I had the address of a furnished room where I had been advised to stay, since the landlady had once lived in Nerchinsk Zavod and should remember my father. Nevertheless, when we said good-bye, the ballerina insistently thrust on me a little paper with her landlady's address. Getting a cabby I went to find the furnished rooms. It turned out that the building was under major repair, and there were no furnished rooms at all. I had to go to the ballerina's address on Izmailovsky Prospect. The old landlady (Katerina Filippovna) met me with such a genial and welcoming face that I immediately felt confidence in her. She already knew about me from the ballerina. From our conversation it became clear that she had no free rooms. In one unoccupied room she had a private dining room; about ten railway engineering students and three petty officials from some department came there to eat dinner. She could give me full board (breakfast, dinner, and supper), and I could sleep on the divan in the dining room, and could study, when the dining room was occupied, in the room of her daughter, a teacher, who was rarely home during the day. I agreed since the cost of everything was thirty-five rubles and, of the fifty rubles Father had assigned me per month, I had fifteen rubles left for petty expenses.

2.

Student Life in St. Petersburg and France

Busy, noisy streets greeted Anna Nikolaevna when she arrived in St. Petersburg at the end of her month-long journey across the Russian Empire in the fall of 1894. At first glance it seemed that everyone was trying to sell something to someone. Boys hawked newspapers and newly printed broadsides, encouraging patrons to buy this or that product, to attend this or that meeting or performance. Peasant women stood in the market places, at the railroad stations and on busy crossroads. Some proffered hand-knit gloves, mittens, and stockings for sale, others foodstuffs such as milk and hot pies. *Muzhiki,* the bearded men from the countryside in their long jackets or caftans and ill-fitting footwear, sold handmade brooms, brushes, and baskets, game birds and rabbits, calling out their prices and extolling the quality of their goods. Finding herself in a large city for the first time in her life, Anna Nikolaevna walked through this crowd looking for a certain address and a place to stay.

The city where she had come to study was in the throes of intense growth and change. Already the largest city in the empire, St. Petersburg had a population of more than 1.25 million people by 1897, when Russia conducted its first national census.[1] Home to the Imperial family and the court, it was the administrative and financial heart of the empire, as well as a center of heavy industry. St. Petersburg was also the most vibrant intellectual and artistic center of the empire. Here were situated the Academy of Sciences and myriad institutions of higher education. Avant-garde trends in literature, theater, music and dance, and fine arts thrived in St. Petersburg, where Anna Nikolaevna visited art galleries, museums, and historic sites, and attended the opera and ballet with her fellow students.

She also entered into a world of intense debate about political, social, and cultural issues. As this chapter indicates, women's rights and revolutionary politics were twin issues that dominated student circles. Discussions of women's rights took place in a climate that was more favorable to women in some ways than in Western Europe. To be sure, in late Imperial Russia educated women still suffered severe inequalities compared to men. The opportunities for leading an independent life were limited; as Anna Nikolaevna herself remarks, in towns like Nerchinsk Zavod young women were expected to marry and become mothers. Unmarried women were under their fathers' control and, like Anna Nikolaevna, had to obtain their permission to travel or to attend school. Married women enjoyed no more freedom under the law; they were not allowed to have an independent passport, to take a job without their husband's permission, to live separately from their husband (unless he was sentenced to exile), or to sue for divorce save for cases of adultery or desertion. Both Russian law and society's norms required women to obey their husbands, to honor and take care of them and their children.

At the same time, from the eighteenth century Russian women had enjoyed wide-ranging rights to control their own property and to carry out legal proceedings in their own name. Russia arguably also led Europe in secondary and higher education for women. Anna Nikolaevna belonged to the generation of women, born during the period of political reform and social activism under Emperor Alexander II (1855–1881), who benefited from the opening of unprecedented educational opportunities for women at this time. This chapter of the memoir provides valuable insights into both the experiences and thoughts of young women pursuing higher education and professional careers in the late nineteenth century.

Access to higher education for Russian women opened slowly. Disapproving of the numbers seeking higher education, Alexander II forbade women to attend university lectures in 1863. Some went abroad, particularly to Zurich, Switzerland, where they were admitted to the university and earned degrees, many in medicine. Impatient with the lack of opportunity in Russia, a group of prominent women social activists, supported by professors committed to women's education and by some high officials, including the Minister of War Dmitri Milyutin, united to open up higher education for women. They persuaded the tsar with their arguments, their position strengthened by the sizable donations they collected for women's education and the fact that many professors were willing to teach without remuneration. In 1876 Alexander II allowed the opening of "Higher Courses for Women" at all Russian universities, including those known as the Bestuzhev Courses in St. Petersburg. However, alarmed by the rebellious mood among students and the threat women's education posed to a conservative social order, Alexander III (1881–1894) ordered the higher women's courses closed. Only the Bestuzhev Courses, which Anna Nikolaevna attended from 1894 to 1895, stayed open, and then, in the mid-1890s, the ban was lifted.

Women seeking a medical education encountered additional obstacles. As in Europe and the United States, government officials, educators, and physicians voiced serious objections to exposing women, with their smaller brains and frail health, to such unsuitable subjects as anatomy and physiology. But aspiring women doctors like Anna Nikolaevna were not to be denied. Even without state permission, they attended courses in St. Petersburg until 1863, when the government forbade them from even auditing courses. Women students then went abroad, especially to Zurich, where a significant number combined their studies with radical politics. With the support of Milyutin and liberal professors, the Higher Women's Medical Courses opened in 1872 in St. Petersburg. The courses were closed in 1882 in the wake of the assassination of Alexander II by radical students, and they remained closed when Anna Nikolaevna arrived in St. Petersburg from Siberia in 1894; they finally reopened in 1897 under the new name of the Women's Medical Institute, offering a five-year program leading to a medical degree and the right to practice.

Like her predecessors in the 1860s and 1870s, Anna Nikolaevna went abroad when she could not obtain a medical education at home, first to Paris and then to the University of Nancy. Illuminated in this chapter are the wide-ranging reactions of Russians to what they observed in Western Europe and the comparisons they continually made, both positive and negative, with their native country. Having traveled on her own from Siberia all the way to France, Anna Nikolaevna was surprised to discover unfamiliar restrictions on women's independence. As we learn from her memoir, young Russian women felt free to walk about in the cities and to travel abroad without a chaperone. When Anna Nikolaevna and her friends arrived in Nancy and looked for inexpensive housing, they were suspected of being prostitutes; respectable French girls did not travel and live alone. They were also astonished to find that there were no French women students in their classes. Married French women, Anna Nikolaevna also relates with indignation, did not have the right to wages that they themselves earned. Clearly Russian women had more rights and higher expectations than their Western European sisters.

When the Women's Medical Institute opened in 1897 Anna Nikolaevna hurried back to St. Petersburg to enter. Her memoir reflects that she was very homesick for Russia at this time. She may also have found living abroad much more expensive than living in Russia. She registered in the first class of the Institute where she found her studies easy, for she already knew the material from her stay in Nancy. This left her free to get involved in the restless student political life within and outside the Institute.

The St. Petersburg Anna Nikolaevna returned to in 1897 was a city in turmoil. Critics of the autocratic government spanned the political spectrum from conservative monarchists on the Right to revolutionaries and anarchists on the Left. Conservatives sought stricter control over political dissidence as well as ethnic and religious minorities, especially the Finns, Poles, and Jews. Liberal opponents of the autocracy shared disgust for its inefficient and corrupt bureaucracy, repression of civil rights, failure to improve the lot of either workers or peasants, and suffocating regulation of industry and local government. On the Left Russia had a range of socialist movements advocating the overthrow of the autocracy, which particularly attracted students. Some young people tended toward radical populism, whose socialist teachings found inspiration in the collectivist Russian peasant community and the example of the student radicals of the 1860s and 1870s. Others were attracted to Marxist "scientific socialism." Among students in St. Petersburg, the Marxist assertion that the rise of the working class was historically inevitable drew special force from the obvious and rapid economic and social changes taking place there, with its giant factories, thousands of peasant immigrants, and new class of industrial working poor. Socialist students dedicated themselves to raising the consciousness of workers and organizing them for more effective political resistance to the government and industrialists.

Anna Nikolaevna became a student leader at the Women's Medical Institute and also regularly attended the meetings of a Siberian regional mutual assistance association, or *zemliachestvo*, organized by her two brothers, Innokenty and Afanasy, both university students.[2] She also explicitly identifies herself in the memoir as a Marxist.[3] As her political activity expanded, she came to play a leading role in a sympathy strike at the Institute in 1901, called to support students at Kiev University. As a result, she was suspended from the Institute in May 1901 after four years of study, just one year short of completing her degree, and exiled home to Siberia for a year.

Medical school and political activities brought Anna Nikolaevna into contact with numerous other young people, including potential boyfriends. A short piece written after she completed her main memoir, entitled "Young Men," provides a glimpse into the lighter side of Russian student life, with its romantic intrigues tinged by politics. She describes the attractions or lack thereof of young men she met, and her own romantic inclinations. She lets us laugh ruefully with her as she restrains herself from caressing the luxuriant wavy hair of one for whom she yearns even after his political duplicity is made clear to her. Back home in Nerchinsk Zavod, she asserts her unwillingness to follow social convention, saying no to suitor Lovitsky and the humdrum life of the wife of a mining engineer in far eastern Siberia, and refusing a frivolous army officer who lacked the seriousness she sought in a partner. As we will see in the next chapter, she returned to St. Petersburg to finish her degree, but only after she married a fellow exile, a doctor and educator who shared many of her life goals.

MEMOIRS

St. Petersburg

The next morning [after arriving in St. Petersburg] I set off for Professor Yakubovich, carrying the box with Melshin's manuscript and letter. I mounted the main, carpeted staircase with trepidation. The professor himself opened the door to my ring. The cold expression on his face did not change when I explained that I had brought him a letter and package from far away, from his brother. He led me into his office. Carelessly casting aside the box with the manuscript and reading the letter, he furrowed his brow. It was clear that the tie with his politically outcast brother did not give him joy. When I told him the goal of my trip, he announced in irritation, "What stupidity! To go so far without finding out whether the Medical Institute is open! Actually, it is so simple, like drinking a glass of water. The Medical Institute is not open and no one knows when it will be!"

I was dismayed, and said: "It's hard for news to get to us in Transbaikal. I thought about going to the Higher Women's Courses if the Medical Institute had not yet opened." To this I heard his harsh answer: "And you won't get in there. They take only those who have finished the gymnasium, and you have only finished some sort of Irkutsk institute, with an unknown program." All his harsh words, pronounced in an irritated tone, were like the blows of a fist to my head. I felt a spasm in my throat; fearing that I would burst into tears in front of him, I stood up, with my voice giving way, said, "Farewell," and went quickly to the door. He evidently noticed my distress, and said in a softer tone, "My sister will be sorry not to meet you. She is not home today. Come see us another time." I did not answer. Then he followed me out, after I had already gone down the stairs, and asked for my address. I gave it without turning around so that he would not see that tears were already coursing down my cheeks.

After leaving there I went directly to Vasilevsky Island where the Higher Women's Courses were located. Lost in depressing thoughts, I did not look around me. There, contrary to my expectations, they were interested in me, looked at my outstanding school record, and took me without any further ado. I enrolled in the physical-mathematics department, where they also taught natural sciences, as I thought that this branch was closer to medicine than history and literature. My spirits rose immediately. On the way back, sitting on a horse-drawn tram (there weren't [electric] trams yet, then), I admired the Neva [River] with the majestic bridge across it and the beautiful buildings and little steamboats scurrying about with passengers along the Fontanka [River]. Everything was interesting and joyful.

So began my student life. Attendance at lectures filled my life. I mastered the content of the lectures easily. I acquired some girlfriends among the students. Coming home from classes, I would find a noisy company of students and officials in the dining room. At the beginning, every day during dinner there was a stormy debate over the Olga Palem affair.[4] At that time there was great discussion in all the newspapers of the trial concerning the murder of a student by the girl O. Palem. The young girl considered herself the student's wife. One day he grossly insulted her. In a temper she snatched his revolver from him and fired. Everyone was interested in whether the court would punish the girl strictly or leniently. At dinner some would be for leniency, others for the strictest possible punishment. I remember how one chubby railway engineering student cried out: "If they are lenient with her, then we'll all get shot." I found it disgusting to look at him.

One of the officials, handsome, elegantly dressed, with a diamond pin in his tie, also supported the strictest punishment. He often stayed to talk to me after dinner. His name was De Mor. He told me about himself and that his forefathers were distinguished Spaniards. His father became Russified and had an estate near Moscow. One day, when we two were together, he began to say in a languid voice that he felt unhappy that he was single. "When I come home from work tired," he said, "no one meets me, no one caresses me," and so on. I was not disposed to a conversation on the theme of love. Remembering his attitude to the girl O. Palem, I said, "I would recommend that you get a dog." He looked at me in astonishment. I explained: "A dog would be tender and would not make any moral demands on you." He burst out laughing and, changing his tone, confessed that he had made declarations of love to women countless times in his life, beginning with housemaids and ending with society ladies, and was so practiced in it that he knew ahead of time what answer he would get from each one. "Only I have had no experience till now with Siberian women and did not expect such an answer from you." After that he switched over to courting a young widow, who had come from Moscow to have a good time and to become acquainted with the sights of Petersburg. The widow and her sister dined at our landlady's. On Sundays De Mor was their guide, and I joined them to visit museums and such. The ballerina had given me tickets to the theater and sometimes took me with her backstage. Thus I heard the opera *Aida* for the first time, standing in the wings. The artists went past me in their make-up which spoiled the totality of the impression.

In work and play the year passed by as though a dream. In the spring [of 1895] I passed all the exams successfully and was promoted to the second year. But here I began to feel dissatisfaction. My aspiration to a medical career was not moving ahead. No one heard anything about the opening of the Medical Institute. On learning that women could get a medical education abroad, I wrote Father a persuasive letter and asked him for permission to go to Paris. I spent the summer months in a relief team for the starving in Ufa Province. Our privately funded team of four women students was sent to the Tatar village Bolshoe Ibraikino. There we saw a terrible scene: in many houses whole families were lying around, swollen from starvation; others with spiritless faces barely dragged themselves along the street. Our team was richly supplied with food. We opened a cafeteria and divided the village into four districts so one of us could care for the sick in each district. We reaped satisfaction out of seeing how quickly our very ill patients got better, stood up on their feet, and, in many cases, whereas during our first visit we had written "all are lying swollen, barely alive," shortly we would find the house locked and neighbors explaining that everybody had gone into the fields to work.

On my return to Petersburg I received a letter from Father and permission to go abroad.

My brother, Innokenty, entered the university at this time. He helped me to get ready to go abroad. He obtained my exit visa. On the eve of my departure we had our picture taken so as to send Father a postcard.

Recollections of Life Abroad

At the station for foreign travel, my passenger train ticket in hand, I sat down at a little table to have a cup of coffee. A German officer sat down at the same little table. A conversation started up, in mixed languages. I knew more French words than German. He didn't know French well. Learning that I was going from distant Siberia to Paris to study, he took an interest in my fate. He himself was going on the express to Berlin and advised me to pay extra for the express and not to wait for the passenger train. With the large number of trains, I was worried about getting on the right one. His help resolved my problem. The porters and conductors were not sociable and were not inclined to talk to foreigners. The train traveled at one hundred kilometers an hour and, in spite of that, moved gently, without shaking or jolting. In contrast I remembered the train from Tyumen, which had evoked my admiration at that time, its car shaking with the bumps. In Berlin my accidental fellow traveler helped me to buy a ticket and get on a train to Munich. There I had to transfer again and wait several hours. At the station I heard Russian spoken at one of the tables, guessed they were students, and approached them. One of the students offered to show me the sights of Munich, and I went with him. I was struck by the cleanliness of the streets and sidewalks, even more than with the beauty of the buildings and monuments. It seemed as if everything was washed till it shone. The student told me that thanks to the cleanliness in Munich there was absolutely no one ill with typhoid fever so medical students had to study the disease by taking trips to Russia. At the French border I boarded an ordinary passenger train, and it reminded me of Russian trains. The trains didn't arrive exactly on time, and there was some unforeseen stop in the fields. On the other hand, the conductors were remarkable for their courtesy: they asked politely for tickets to be shown, begged your pardon for disturbing you, and so on.

With our arrival in Paris, on the city outskirts, I was amazed by the heaps of vegetables and miscellaneous wares laid out on the sidewalks; you could buy things without going into the stores. I saw the center of the city considerably later. From Petersburg I had the address of rooms where Russian students usually stayed and a letter to the student Smetanina requesting help in getting me settled. I got a room. I did not meet any of this landlady's Russian students as it was vacation time. So I went straight to Smetanina, to the address on the letter. To my chagrin, it turned out that she had gone to her dacha in the suburbs of Paris. After I learned the address of the dacha I set out on a steamboat on the Seine River. I found Smetanina in bed; she had just given birth to a baby and was not in the mood for me. Nonetheless she informed me of how to fill out an application to the university, where to turn it in, and so on. Returning on the steamboat I discovered to my horror that my wallet had disappeared from my coat pocket. It contained one hundred rubles, which I had calculated would take care of two months in Paris.[5] It was lucky that I had a few francs in my bag with which I could return to Paris and, by eating meagerly, I could last a few days. Part of this money went for a telegram to Father with the request to wire money. The cheerless days dragged on. In the restaurant I bought only boiled potatoes, as they were the cheapest dish. In a gloomy mood I walked half-starving through the streets of Paris, and it seemed strange to me that all around I heard laughter and gay conversations among the people passing by. Parisians in general amazed me with their gay sociability; even in horse-drawn trams chance passengers entered into general conversation. That didn't happen among the sullen Petersburg public.

An unusual spectacle distracted me from my personal depression. It was election eve and there was a street battle between the different parties. There were posters everywhere; multicolored leaflets were being distributed, telling you to vote for certain persons. On the street corners meetings were held and orators gave speeches. "That's what being a republic means," I thought, "At home in Russia the tsarist power would never allow anything similar." I couldn't get involved in political questions as I was engaged exclusively with my goal of getting a medical education.

My application for acceptance to the medical department lay stalled in the commissariat because they were expecting a change in ministers because of the elections. There were rumors that the admission of foreigners into the university would be forbidden, because foreigners were crowding out French students in the lectures and laboratories. This new obstacle on my path upset me deeply.

During repeated visits to the commissariat I met and came to know three girls who had also come from Russia to enter medical school. I was very glad that now I was not alone in this huge alien city. In answer to our inquiries at the commissariat they told us that, for foreigners to be allowed admission, we had to pass exams in Latin and Greek beforehand. We had known about this earlier and had already prepared ourselves in Russia, but here we would have to take the exam in French. We jointly hired a tutor—the Russian emigrant Stankevich who had already been living in Paris several years. We had heard about him, how he was very hard up and living only on what he made from such lessons. Meeting daily for study in the tutor's poor quarters we became very close to one another, we became like family.

Coming from different cities, from different circumstances, we were united by our common goal and the need to overcome obstacles in our path. There was Mariya Stupina from Kharkov. Her exterior amazed Parisians; she was very fat, with short hair, a broad, good-natured face and almost always had a cigarette in her teeth. She attracted the attention of passers-by, and frequently little boys on the street ran after her, laughing and pointing at her with their fingers. The good-hearted Stupina was not affected by this. From Kiev there was Emma Braude, short, thin, with a pale, colorless little face, and a skinny little pigtail. In her short brown dress

Fig. 2.1. Anna Zhukova with her fellow Russian students in Nancy, between 1895 and 1897; she is seated, first on the right.

she looked like a girl gymnast. Only the pince-nez on her nose gave her some kind of solidity. She was from a Jewish family with many children and little means. In contrast to her was Sonya Ilina, the daughter of a Moscow factory owner, a tall shapely blonde with luxuriant hair and a rosy, slightly snub-nosed face, very sociable and gay. After about two weeks we all took the exam in classical languages. The least prepared of all of us was Stupina. I remember an amusing incident, how on the exam she translated a passage from the Greek about the death of some hero. The examiner ironically said: "Excuse me, mademoiselle, he was not killed on this page, but on the following one." Stupina had to go to the tutor again, and she passed the exam the second time. At last the turnover in the ministry took place and, again after a long wait, we heard the order: "Foreigners may only enter provincial universities." The four of us decided to go to the city of Nancy, on the border of Germany, and therefore closer to Russia. In addition we were told that because of the rivalry with Germany the French government was trying to make this university as good as possible.

Of the sights of Paris, only the Bastille comes clearly to mind. Before the great French Revolution this was a prison where political criminals were held. The exterior of the prison retained its former appearance: you enter a gloomy corridor, pass rows of doors to dark damp cells, and at the end of the corridor there is a small staircase going up, you climb up, and open the door, and suddenly . . . you seem to be on a brightly lit balcony, with a view onto Bastille Square at the moment when the Bastille was taken by the revolutionary populace. What excited faces, the triumph of victory! The panorama is done so well, you are fully persuaded that you are standing on the balcony and that you indeed are seeing not a picture but the real square with a living crowd of revolutionary people.[6]

While I was in Paris, the conclusion of the alliance with Russia was on the political horizon.[7] Meetings were held, and the newspapers ran a lot of articles about the significance of the alliance with Russia. Together with my girlfriends I went to a celebratory meeting in a large theater where, after speeches about the alliance with Russia, a play about life in Siberia was put on. It was obvious that the author concocted this play hastily, knowing neither Russia nor Siberia. The hero of the play, Michel Strogov (his name probably confused with the name Stroganov) goes to Siberia. At the postal station he is met by the stationmaster in a tailcoat and a top hat. The hero orders *pelmeni* and *kvas* at the buffet.[8] He is brought this and that in little plates, and he eats, using a fork and knife. There were a lot of such absurdities, and we laughed a lot. I still remember an antireligious demonstration that students staged against a Catholic procession going along the street, with whistles, meows, and so on. This astonished us, as it seemed strange.

Another time we saw an interesting spectacle on the street. I don't remember which day is the traditional holiday for laundresses. The best laundress (who also had to be beautiful and moral) was elected tsaritsa. She was dressed in a magnificent white dress with a crown on her head. They put a throne on a decorated chariot and, with music playing, drove the tsaritsa of laundresses through the streets. Big crowds greeted her with good wishes, and threw flowers into the chariot and packages with some sort of presents. They say that this procession always ends with a ball and refreshments.

Life in the City of Nancy

On our arrival in town Braude and I ran into difficulty finding a room. Ilina's rich mother immediately settled Sonya in one of the professors' apartments. Nor was Stupina strapped for funds, and, with Ilina's help, she also found a room easily. Emma Braude's parents sent her only twenty-five rubles a month, and you could not live on that kind of money. Somehow it just happened that the two of us got together. Father sent me fifty rubles. On seventy-five rubles the two of us could live modestly, but our difficulty was that people distrusted us. In a provincial city at that time only girls of "easy virtue" could walk about freely. Honorable girls had to be accompanied by older women. When we saw a little card in a window that a room was for rent and rang the bell, the landlady, on opening the door, viewed us suspiciously, and asked: "Vous êtes des femmes vulgaires?" (Are you girls of easy virtue?) Despite our explanation that we were Russian students, the door in front of us slammed shut. After several failures, we finally found a room in an attic with a sloping ceiling, a little window, and an iron stove in the middle of the room. We were content with this, even though later it turned out that the room was so cold that the ink on our table froze on winter nights.

We all went together to the university the first day and modestly took the last places in the auditorium. Before this we had learned that a new order had been received: before entering the medical faculty all students had to pass a one-year course in the natural sciences (physics, chemistry, botany, and zoology). This new delay in our path to medicine did not particularly distress us. We had been late getting to Nancy; classes had already been going on for about a month. We had to familiarize ourselves with scientific French. I was helped a lot by the fact that I had studied for a year in Petersburg in a physics and math department. I quickly mastered the language and began to take lecture notes in French. The others used my notes.

Among the students there was not a single French woman, but there were two women among the one hundred Bulgarian students. Bulgaria did not have its own university then and so, according to an agreement, the country sent one hundred students to the medical school annually. For some reason we didn't get to know the Bulgarians; we lived isolated in our little Russian colony. The French students took us seriously, but, with young Emma, they sometimes allowed themselves some mischief, either hiding her hat in the cloakroom or dangling her galoshes on the hanging lamp. One of the students would have begun to court Ilina in earnest, but she laughed at him and said that she would rather marry a bad Russian than a Frenchman, even if the Frenchman were a better man. Our academic life quickly settled into a routine. On our way home after class, Emma and I went to the little store where a horse's head stood out vividly on the signboard and bought a piece of cheap horsemeat. At home we cooked our "beefsteak" on the iron stove. It could be chewed only with difficulty. For supper we bought salad or herring. Thus we stayed on our budget without any deficit. Ilina tried to offer us money for better food, but we proudly refused handouts.

At the university I particularly liked the practical work with the microscope in botany and zoology. I remember how once I was lost in admiration of a beautiful picture of cell division. In order to share my impressions with Stupina, I tore myself away from the microscope and unexpectedly found myself face to face with the professor who had come to my desk unheard. Evidently my enraptured expression attracted his attention, and he offered me work in his office. When I came to his office the next day after classes I found one of the best students there. The professor gave us both a job—to separate frogs' eggs from the surrounding mucus without harming them. The other student did it successfully, but no matter how hard I tried I damaged the eggs. Convinced of my clumsiness, I was so embarrassed by this that I stopped going to the professor's office.

From childhood I loved to draw and managed better with a pencil than with instruments. In practical classes we were often given the assignment of drawing this or that laboratory preparation, and my drawings always received a good evaluation. In French schools a great deal of attention was given to drawing, and all the French students knew how to draw. Stupina drew the best of all the students; she was the daughter of an artist, and her drawings stood out for their fine, artistic execution. Emma, however, did not have even the most elementary skills in drawing and held her pencil awkwardly. I remember how once we had the assignment of preparing a spider and drawing the structure of its nervous system. For Emma this was completely unfeasible: she drew the outline of the spider as a preschooler would draw the sun—a circle and, around it, little short lines. In order to rescue Emma, I had to draw for her and slip it to her unobserved. While she was poorly prepared in natural sciences, Emma was the strongest of us on political issues. When the Jewish girl Struzer came to us for a time from the University of Lille, we began to have heated debates in the evenings, especially about the agrarian question in connection with the possibility of revolution in Russia.[9] One time their debates became such a shouting match that the landlady, hearing us downstairs, came up to our attic and left the door ajar, afraid, apparently, that the shouting would turn into a fight. In the morning she looked on with astonishment as last night's enemies went harmoniously to class. I understood little of politics, giving myself completely to university work.

Thus winter passed. In the spring I alone of our colony decided to take all the exams. The others put the exams off till the fall; at the same time they greatly sympathized with me, saying that I had to support the honor of the Russian students. The whole time that I was preparing for the exams they touchingly looked after me, fixing food, cleaning my dress and shoes.

I justified their hopes; later one of the assistants told me that I had gotten the highest marks in all the subjects and was supposed to get the appropriate award, but at the faculty meeting it was suggested to the professors that they lower my grade so as not to place a foreigner higher than the French students. They decided to give me a certificate of merit. I did not attend the ceremony and did not pick it up. All my thoughts were directed at leaving as quickly as possible for Russia for vacation.

From a letter I knew that my beloved aunt Demidova (my mother's sister) had gone from Chita to Oranienbaum, where her husband had been sent on business.[10] She was waiting for me there. We were all homesick; everything in France seemed foreign and strange. The grown-up daughters of the [French] professor where Ilina lived answered the question: "Why can't you go out on the street without an older person?" by saying: "Oh! We would risk not getting married!"

We were even more amazed by the position of a married woman; if the woman worked independently in some enterprise or another, her wages were paid only to her husband or to her only on receipt of a proxy from her husband. Our landlady would relate with delight the story of her niece who was educated in some sort of Catholic boarding school at a convent: "She is so well brought up that she avoids men and will not even sit at the same table with her male cousins."

We lived isolated in our little Russian colony; we always spoke Russian to one another and did little to perfect our conversational French. My departure for Russia was unexpectedly delayed. Ilina announced that she was getting married and absolutely needed all of us to be at her wedding. This was totally unexpected. She had kept secret that she had begun a love affair with Stankevich, who had tutored us for the exam in classical languages. He was pale, thin, and, with a sunken chest, looked ill with tuberculosis. When she told me about the upcoming wedding I exclaimed involuntarily, "Sonya, what are you doing, he's surely consumptive!" She answered with a sweet smile, "But he has a good soul!" It was convincing. If he was actually ill, then Sonya with her wealth would make it possible for him to improve his health. Up to then he had been living impoverished in Paris, on the pennies he earned from lessons. I don't know how Sonya managed to persuade her mother. As the owner of a big silk factory in Moscow, she would hardly take to a son-in-law who was a Russian revolutionary.

Be that as it may, the mother took great pains over the wedding. She tracked down a Russian church in Paris, ordered the groom an expensive suit from the best workshop and her daughter a stylish wedding outfit; she bought us railroad tickets to Paris and organized a reception there in an expensive restaurant. In the church, besides us, there assembled a crowd of curious Parisians. Obviously the contrast between the appearance of the bridegroom and the bride astonished everyone. In the crowd you heard talk: "The bridegroom looks like a corpse, he must be a millionaire, and the mother, seduced by his riches, is giving up her beautiful daughter, blooming with health, for those riches." How they would have been amazed to know that everything was the other way around.

The wedding over, I rush to Russia on German express trains. I am excited, approaching the Russian border. At the border station I see a soldier in a Russian uniform, and, not fully sure that I will hear Russian speech, I ask: "Tell me, where can I get my luggage?" In answer, I hear, "And where'd ya hand it in?"[11] The country speech was like music to my ears. I was—in Russia . . . I arrived at my aunt's, pale, thin from intense studying and bad food. When I fell asleep in the middle of the day, Aunt Lyolichka, worrying, came to see if I was still alive. With a summer under her solicitous care, I quickly recovered and in the fall again went to Nancy.

Now at last I had reached medicine. At the center of my studies was the study of anatomy using cadavers. We worked in a large, beautiful hall with a glass ceiling. After a year of our modest life in Nancy attitudes toward Russian students had improved, and Emma and I found a wonderful room without trouble. In the spring we successfully passed the exams for the first year of medical school. At the same time I learned that the Woman's Medical Institute would open in the fall in Petersburg. Stupina and I applied for admission, although only the first year was being opened. My brother, Innokenty, jokingly informed me, "On the list of those admitted appears the name Zhukova, Anna. How happy I am that you are Anna!" Stupina and I decided to make our way back to Russia through Switzerland. We sent our baggage on the railroad and, equipped with a guidebook and alpenstocks, we went by foot through the most picturesque places. At the foot of the peak of the Jungfrau we spent the night in a lonely hotel meant especially for travelers. I remember the beautiful view from the hotel window. Stupina fell ill with angina and went to bed early. I sat for a long time by the open window. Below, in the valley, dark blue night had already fallen, lamps were being lit in the houses, but the snowy peak of the Jungfrau was still brightly lit by the setting sun. Approximately every half hour muffled peals just like distant thunder resounded, the sound of periodic avalanches.[12]

Part of our route lay on the shore of the Vierwaldstätter See [Lake Lucerne]. The beauty of the view thrilled us. The somber, historic castle of Chillon towered over the tiny little island. A little bridge linked it with the shore. For a fee we went to look at the castle's interior. The lower floor was the prison where formerly prisoners had languished, fettered by iron chains to stone pillars. Around each pillar tracks remained in the stone floor, circular depressions made by the trudging of unhappy prisoners. The guide who explained this to us was an elegant girl in a light, white dress; against the dark background of the prison she looked like a fairy from a fairy tale. On the upper floor was a bright hall where once knights had banqueted, and, in the middle of the hall, a huge hearth on which the knights might roast a whole lamb. On the entire route, shown in detail in our guidebook, the local inhabitants of Switzerland used tourists to support themselves. When travelers arrive in one place an old man, a flutist, plays a pretty little melody on the flute that then echoes in the mountains seventeen times, loudly at first and then softly and ever more softly. Elsewhere girls sing while sitting on ice benches in a glacier cavern.

With our trip through Switzerland Stupina and I finished our life abroad.

Recollections of Student Life in Petersburg (1897–1903)

About three years had passed since I had left Nerchinsk Zavod with the vague hope of entering the Medical Institute that year—and only now did the doors of the Institute open before me. These three years had not passed without purpose. I had seen a great deal and acquired much knowledge. I was grateful to Father for the opportunity to study. What sort of prospects did I have in Nerchinsk Zavod? I could marry an engineer. My position obliged me to. Mining engineers received huge salaries. Where could they spend them? Engineers' wives ordered stylish dresses from Paris, held evening card parties at home in turn, competing with one another in the richness of their hospitality, who had the finest fruit liqueurs and wines, and so on. I had a different path before me.

To reduce the cost to my father, I decided to earn something in the summer before the beginning of classes. The Sapozhnikov family from Irkutsk asked me to tutor their little girl and to teach her French. They lived in a dacha in the village of Izhory on the shore of the Gulf of Finland, and I spent a pleasant summer with their agreeable family. When classes began at the Medical Institute, only the first year course opened, and I had to go through in Russian what I had already passed in French. It was easy, and without hurting my studies I could spend a lot of time on social work. At the first organizational meeting of women students I was elected deputy (elder), and from then on, every year of the courses, I was reelected. Smirnova was elected second deputy. Modest and serious, she was immediately liked and trusted. We had a lot of work. We had to eliminate problems in the recently opened dormitory, cafeteria, classrooms, and so on. The Medical Institute was opened with private funds collected through the initiative of a group from the progressive intelligentsia. Among them was Varvara Ivanovna, Baroness Ikskul, who after the opening of the Institute looked after it, reviewing all its needs. She came to the Institute in her own stylish carriage but more often sent for me and Smirnova to call on her on business. After classes we had to drag ourselves along on foot from the Petersburg Side to Sergievskaya Street where she had her stone, two-story private residence. Discussion of business often dragged on till nighttime. At the end a lackey brought us a tray with spice cakes and tea in elegant Japanese teacups. We needed more substantial food. On the way home, hungry and tired, we tramped through the mud and criticized the aristocratic baroness's attitude toward us. In all of Petersburg at that time the revolutionary mood could be felt; it was reflected as well among students. Shortly after the beginning of classes we organized a strike against the chemistry teacher, Zalessky, who had made mistakes from the first lectures and did not please the students. As a result of the strike someone else replaced him.

In organizing a mutual assistance fund, we came into conflict with the director. He wanted to reserve for himself the right to give out assistance.

Fig. 2.2. Students at the Women's Medical Institute, St. Petersburg, between 1897 and 1901; Anna Zhukova is the second from the right.

We claimed firmly that only we ourselves could figure out who was the most in need. We knew that the director's choices would be determined by political reliability.

Our physics course was taught by Prince Golitsyn. After two months of classes he received some high post or other and had to leave us. The director suggested that we organize a send-off for him and thank him for the honor of attending his lectures. We sharply refused. The director Anrep was liberally inclined; avoiding great conflicts, he sought compromise. Once, on some occasion, he told us: "As a man I sympathize with students, but as director I have to protest!" Like many students I merely wished the overthrow of the autocracy and did not think about what should come after. I gained a more serious revolutionary temperament in our Transbaikal association [*zemliachestvo*]. *Zemliachestva,* associations of people from the same region for the material aid of those in need, were officially permitted in all higher education institutions. Transbaikalians, under the flag of regional association meetings, organized a Marxist circle. Among the organizers were my brothers, Innokenty and Afanasy. The meetings ran according to the following agenda:

1) Lecture or chapter reading from Marx's *Capital*
2) Discussion, debate

3) Tea drinking (tea with crackers)

4) Choral singing

There was never any dancing or drinking. The songs we sang usually had a revolutionary theme:

1. *Boldly, Comrades, in step*
2. *Break the fetters, set me free, I'll teach you to love freedom*
3. *I sit behind bars*
4. *From the country, the country far away*
5. *Dubinushka*, with a revolutionary ending.[13] And others.

The organizer of the chorus was always my brother, Innokenty. Members of the circle were not only fellow Transbaikalians but also people from other regional associations through strict recommendations of circle members. Thus we took a Jew from Minsk, who had studied Marxist literature seriously and readily gave lectures in the circle. His lectures were notable for their dry, boring presentation. It was hard for many members of the circle to grasp the sense of the completely new, profound ideas of Marxism. But the enthusiasm of the organizers made everyone pull themselves together and pay strict attention.

I remember a little incident along this line. At first some women students came to the meeting with some kind of needlework. One of the organizers, noticing this, exclaimed indignantly: "We read Marx's *Capital* to them and they sew skirts!" From that time on needlework disappeared. My brother Afanasy lectured on "The Intelligentsia: Servant of Capitalists," and it went in a very lively fashion. This topic touched the future intelligentsia to the quick. Furious debates erupted. The lecturer developed the Marxist view of the structure of the capitalistic state and was unassailable. Another time there were lively debates over the student Markova's lecture. By some chance she had traveled to Berlin and had become acquainted with Bernstein's teachings there.[14] Bernstein's compromise doctrine elicited a sharply negative reaction from the students. After a hot debate the speaker herself agreed with them. No matter how the lectures went, after them sympathy for the workers in their struggle with the capitalists stayed in one's soul. The choral singing of revolutionary songs heightened the feeling, and we dispersed after the meeting in a state of excitement. It seemed to me personally that up to that time I had been wandering in some sort of fog; now Marxism gave me solid ground under my feet. The regularity of the development of nature and society led me to the thought that there must also be a dialectical regularity in the development of the human psyche. Questions of the psyche had interested me earlier. I attended the lectures of Professor Vvedensky, considered one of the best psychologists in Petersburg, but they didn't satisfy me.[15]

When interest in our own lecturers was exhausted, the organizers of the circle decided to invite the then Legal Marxists among the professors to our secret apartment. The students brought, by cab, Peter Struve, Tugan Baranovskii, and Pavel N. Milyukov (for some reason he was considered a Marxist) in turn.[16] The imported orator gave a short lecture on a chosen topic, after which the students asked questions, he answered, and the same students conducted him safely away. After their departure came the usual agenda of tea and choral singing.

In addition to professors we decided to invite A. M. Gorky.[17] Things didn't go so smoothly with him. Clearly he found no point in giving such presentations before students. He refused for a long time; persuaded only with difficulty, he was brought along. With a sullen expression he entered the room, crowded to capacity with students, sat in the chair prepared for him, leaned his elbows on the table, and rested his head on his hand. An uncomfortable silence ensued. One of the students, wishing to break the silence, asked the awkward question, "Which party's program do you follow in your novels?" Gorky scowled even more and answered sharply, "I do not write according to anyone's program." Again there was silence, even heavier than the first. Finally, a student well acquainted with Gorky's works began to talk about types of tramps, about the play *The Lower Depths*.[18] Gorky livened up, and an interesting conversation began.

That was the last meeting of the circle. Shortly after this a student general strike began. The immediate cause was the drafting of some Kiev students into the army because of some sort of demonstration.[19] One after another the Petersburg higher educational institutions announced a strike, demanding the return of the drafted students. Disturbances began even in our Medical Institute. We were already in our fourth year, and we organized a meeting of all the levels. The anxious administration inspired our group of reactionary students. At the meeting the latter spoke out sharply against the strike, saying, "Women's medical education is not yet well established. Private individuals, the founders, succeeded only with great difficulty in getting permission to open our Medical Institute. If we join a political strike our institute will be closed." We objected, pointing to women doctors' social role, and said, "Does Russia need such women doctors, who, in a difficult political moment, will say, 'it's no concern of mine? We're only here to get our diplomas,'" and so on. As a result of stormy debates, a huge majority of the students voted for the strike. A strike committee was elected which, in addition to me and Smirnova, included the excellent orators Peskova and Lavrova. The strike began, and we remained on strike for as long as all the higher educational institutions were on strike. It was spring. When the strike ended we began to get ready for final exams. But suddenly one May morning, when I had only just gotten out of bed, a policeman appeared at my door with an order: "Leave Petersburg in twenty-four hours and go home for one year." I was astounded; yet another obstacle on my road to medical work! I told the policeman that I could not sign that I would obey within twenty-four hours since my journey was long, I had no money, and a request to my father about sending money for the trip home would take a long time.

The policeman said that I should write down the sum I needed for the road and that at 12:00 noon I would receive the money at the gendarme station. Thus I left Petersburg and went to Nerchinsk Zavod.

Expulsions in all the higher educational institutions affected those students whom the gendarmes considered strike ringleaders. Crossing Siberia no longer had to be done on horseback but by railroad, which now went as far as Chita and was under construction to extend further.[20]

My unexpected arrival greatly surprised Father. He was distressed, of course, by my "political unreliability" but did not reproach me. Critical attitudes toward the tsar's power had already begun to penetrate even Nerchinsk Zavod. Father expressed indignation not at the students for striking but at the extravagance of the authorities, who spent state funds giving all those exiled money for the road without requiring repayment.

Father did not live alone. In spite of his sixty years he had married a young woman, a former house servant, and they had had a son, now two years old. My younger brothers, Misha and Kolya, were studying in a gymnasium in Chita.

Young Men

In reviewing my life I recall that I was frivolously attracted to handsome men (like Natasha).[21] I was then a first-year student at the Medical Institute. A medical student, Peter Gavrilovich Sushinsky, moved into the apartment where I, too, was renting a room. I had heard in passing that he had been in prison, from which I concluded that he was a revolutionary.

I liked his appearance right away: a slender, powerful figure, a handsome face and a head of luxuriant wavy hair. His whole figure exuded health, strength, and some kind of male power. We became acquainted. He started coming to my place almost every evening for tea. He always set the theme of our conversations: he spoke about trifles, jested, and told jokes. I was interested in his revolutionary activities, but he evaded any talk about political topics. I explained to myself that this was the caution of a revolutionary. In his joking I sometimes caught tender hints that he liked me. With each day I was more attracted to him. Sometimes the desire rose in me to sit closer to him, to caress his luxuriant hair; but I restrained myself with an effort. One time he began to talk about being in prison and told how he had organized acrobatic exercises that had delighted the prisoners. Thus, for example, he climbed the staircase on his hands, with his legs up in the air. The prison spectators responded, "Well, he's a lord"; "What kind of a lord! Whatever was he sent to prison for?" He never asked anything about me.

I don't know what our acquaintance might have led to, but before long he announced one day that he was being sent to Paris on a mission and was leaving urgently the next day. He did not answer my question, "Who is sending you?" but said that he was paying his own way. I was sad. Before his departure he came to see me and said good-bye tenderly. He asked me to write him and promised that he would write me often. After his departure I felt a heavy grief in my soul. Mornings I hurried to the Medical Institute earlier than necessary to see if there wasn't a letter from him. But no letter came.

Finally a postcard came, with a few phrases about Paris, without his address, and with the closing, "Yours, Peter." Disappointed, I tried to find something tender in that closing. After a number of days, a young girl, very simply dressed, came to my room one evening. She inspired my confidence right away with her sweet face and serious, sad eyes. Without introducing herself, she said that she had received a letter from Peter Gavrilovich from Paris. He was in great need and asked for money to be sent to him; if not money then something in gold. Immediately, without thinking, I got out a gold necklace and brooch—the only gold things I had. I did not want to let this sweet girl leave right away. I sat her down and suddenly, unexpectedly, began to tell her about what I had never spoken to anyone about before, about my acquaintance with P. G., my love, my yearning for him. She said, "You are not alone," and tears trickled down her face. She stood up and left quickly. After she left I began to think, and to have doubts. Why had he not written directly to me, why had he sent her? Was it possible that he had also asked her for money? It was strange to think that this strong, healthy, educated man could not find work and had to ask us for money, knowing how modestly we lived. Was it possible he was a blackmailer? I drove the thought away, but a kind of breach opened up in my soul. I reassured myself by saying that surely he would write to me and explain everything. But no letter came.

Then, after some time, a friend from Irkutsk came to see me early one morning. She studied at the Higher Women's Courses and was a member of the Socialist Revolutionary Party.[22] Knowing that I lived in the same apartment as Sushinsky she had come to warn me. The Party determined that Sushinsky was a provocateur. The other day three comrades were arrested because of an affair that only they and Sushinsky knew about. His very mission to Paris, supposedly on his own means, was in the service of the police. I was staggered and began to tremble all over from agitation. My friend didn't notice anything as she was hurrying to her classes. After her departure I fell on the bed, sick with indignation. What a villain! And I? Like a stupid little girl I fell in love without thinking about what sort of person he was. I was ashamed and my heart was bitter. After getting over my initial feelings, I began to feel relief that now I would no longer suffer by yearning for him. I remembered that today there was a test in anatomy, and I became worried that lately I had prepared poorly for all my tests. I hurriedly went to the Institute. I remember that Professor Batuev asked about the muscles and nerves of the forearm. I was rescued by the fact that in Nancy I had studied anatomy thoroughly. Receiving a grade of excellent, I hurried joyfully out of the auditorium. In the corridor I collided with the fat Stupina with whom I had arrived from France. I seized her by the shoulders and began to dance around her. She looked at me with amazement. I had never displayed such energetic joy after successful exams abroad. She didn't know that I was glad not so much because of the successful exam but most of all because my soul was already lighter. I had no more of the yearning that had been hindering my studies.

My attraction to Sushinsky always seemed absurd to me. I saw his superficiality from his conversations, his frivolous attitude toward life; I understood that we were completely different people; I had not the slightest wish to live with him. Meanwhile, contrary to reason, I yearned for him until disclosure of his baseness destroyed this blind feeling.

The development of my feelings for Doctor Evgeny Vladimirovich Bek took a completely different path.

My past is poor in romantic episodes. In all my youth, until I met Doctor Bek, I had only the two brief crushes that I have already described here (Orlov and Sushinsky). My bitter disillusionment after this made me especially exacting with respect to the moral aspect of a person. When I was my brother Vanya's guest in Kara (that was before his wife's illness) I moved in military circles. There were dances, games of post office, and other things. Officer Ryazanov came often to play chess with me. My brother told me once that Ryazanov wanted to propose to me but couldn't make up his mind. I had no feelings toward him but got along with him well. I thought that he, like my brother, had to be dissatisfied with military service—keeping order at a gold mine where political prisoners worked, people who were suffering because of their convictions. In a conversation on this topic I asked him seriously: "What would you like to be?" He answered: "I would like to be a pretty young lady." With this he ruined himself completely in my eyes.

My desire—to study to become a doctor—suppressed all other interests in me.

In Nerchinsk Zavod it was obvious to all that Engineer Lovitsky was courting me. I resisted his efforts to have an intimate conversation with me, and I feared that he might make an official proposal to me through Father. Then Father would begin to insist on this marriage and would not give me the opportunity to study. But everything turned out happily, and I went away. Several years later I met Lovitsky in Petersburg. From Father's letters I knew that he had married. We met in the theater. I was in the loge with a group of women students. Lovitsky saw me from the parterre and came to see us. We chatted about something. In the next intermission his wife—a middle-aged woman, elegantly dressed—came to see us in the loge. She turned right to me: "Are you Anna Zhukova? My husband said that you were here." Noticeably agitated, she added: "I have never seen my husband in such a happy, excited state, and came to see." . . . Evidently she had felt jealous of me. My modest appearance, it seemed, calmed her down, and having looked me over she went straight away. In medical school I was completely absorbed by my studies and community work, especially when the student disturbances began. Before starting my fifth year I was exiled home for a year from Petersburg, and there I met Doctor Bek.

3.
New Beginnings: Nerchinsk Zavod, St. Petersburg, Aksha

Anna Nikolaevna entered the public realm in the early twentieth century as a doctor, research scholar, teacher, and social activist. Her private life also changed dramatically. She fell in love and married, somewhat to her surprise, the reader of her memoirs surmises. She served in the military as a doctor during the Russo-Japanese War. She bore two daughters, losing the first in infancy but raising the second with joy in a tiny town in eastern Siberia on the Mongolian border. This chapter chronicles her first steps as she leaves student life behind and embarks on her adult career.

Important changes were occurring in Siberia at the opening of the twentieth century. The economy was developing rapidly with the construction of the Trans-Siberian Railroad, which reached Chita, Nerchinsk, and finally Vladivostok on the Pacific Coast in 1903. With the railroad came new towns, manufacturing industries, and workers from European Russia with new skills and new political and social ideas. Equally important was the steadily growing migration of peasants seeking land and more freedom outside the tradition-bound village structure of old European Russia. Thanks to this immigration, Siberia was transformed into a major exporter of grain and dairy products.[1] These changes, however, were slow to reach the eastern Siberian towns where Anna Nikolaevna lived and worked between 1901 and 1912. The town of Nerchinsk Zavod, to which she returned after being exiled for political activity in St. Petersburg, still had only slightly more than three thousand inhabitants; far from the prosperous new farming regions of western Siberia, it was also not on the new railroad line. During the nineteenth century, however, Nerchinsk Zavod had been influenced by the Decembrists and other political exiles. With the turn of the century, news and rumors about mounting political challenges to the tsar reached even here from St. Petersburg and Moscow, fueling discussion and discontent.

The family Anna Nikolaevna returned to in Nerchinsk Zavod was also in flux. Her two older brothers, university students in St. Petersburg, experienced political problems similar to hers—exile and even imprisonment for their radical opinions and activities. Both her older sisters were married, and her father had married his young housekeeper. The biggest change, though, occurred in Anna Nikolaevna's own family status. In 1901 she fell in love and married a young military doctor in Nerchinsk Zavod, Evgeny Vladimirovich Bek, who had been exiled like herself and appointed to a post there far from harm's way. By conventional standards Anna Nikolaevna, at thirty-one years of age, was late in marrying. Like her sisters, most Russian Siberian girls married in their late teens or early twenties. Anna Nikolaevna had spent her twenties pursuing her medical education, and in her free time the ballet and theater, not a husband. Her parents' marriage offered no role model; her mother had not been particularly happy in her married life. However, Anna Nikolaevna's interest in medicine and helping the needy drew her to Bek. He was handsome, well-spoken, and, more important, shared the same goals in life: he wanted to contribute to a better life for the people, and she could envision them working together all their lives. This chapter tells us much about their loving, harmonious partnership.

When Anna Nikolaevna's term of exile came to a close after a year, she left her new husband in Nerchinsk Zavod and went to St. Petersburg for her fifth and final year at the Medical Institute. In 1903 her husband joined her there, sent by his military superiors to update his surgical knowledge. This was not unusual. Teachers, doctors, and other members of the professions regularly attended such courses, often at state expense. Anna Nikolaevna passed her examinations in late 1903 and was awarded her degree in May 1904. Her memoirs pass rapidly over this year, however, and so we learn little of the continuing unrest in the city, the mounting discontent of both educated elites and workers with the repressive Russian government, and the country's economic, social, and political backwardness.

When the Russo-Japanese War began in 1904, both Anna Nikolaevna and her husband became directly involved. As a military doctor Bek had no choice but to serve; he was mobilized and sent to the Manchurian front. Anna Nikolaevna volunteered as a nurse in the same division but, because of her qualifications and the needs of the moment, she was hired to serve as a doctor in a nearby hospital. The Beks treated soldiers who were waiting to join the front or who were part of the retreat. Finding that many of the young soldiers were illiterate, Anna Nikolaevna also organized a literacy circle for them. There was a firmly established tradition among reformers and revolutionaries for teaching basic reading and writing to adult workers and peasants in "Sunday" schools. By educating peasant soldiers Anna Nikolaevna was clearly challenging class norms and the military hierarchy. But she went even further when she challenged an officer for striking a soldier, and then complained about him to the chief surgeon. Her memoir leaves the impression that she enjoyed the controversy that ensued. Her account also makes frequent reference to the ineptitude and corruption of military officers that contributed to Russia's humiliating defeat by Japan.

Striking in its absence, however, is any reference to the revolution that broke out in early 1905 in the midst of the war. Disgusted with the progress of the war and the failure of the tsarist government to accede to their demands for participation in government, Russia's growing liberal opposition renewed its political activity with political banquets and signed declarations in late 1904. Unrest blazed across the country after "Bloody Sunday" on 9 January 1905, when soldiers in the capital fired on an unarmed workers' procession seeking to petition the tsar for better conditions and rights. Across the country outraged Russians organized antigovernment strikes; in Siberia workers in the towns along the new railroad and discontented soldiers returning from defeat in the Far East spread the revolution. Peasants, frustrated by land shortages, low agricultural prices, and the high cost of manufactured goods, burned manor houses and seized land and crops beginning in the autumn of 1905. In October 1905 the tsar capitulated to the demands for civil rights and for limiting the power of the monarchy, and in early 1906 elections were held for Russia's first national elected parliament, the Duma.

The Beks spent at least some of 1905–1906 in St. Petersburg, the epicenter of the revolution. Why does Anna Nikolaevna say nothing about her activities or reactions during this time of crisis for the very government she so actively defied as a student in 1900 and 1901? Perhaps her and her husband's personal pursuits at this time kept them on the margins of national events. They lived with Dr. Bek's sister on the outskirts of the capital. Evgeny Vladimirovich devoted himself to his studies, updating his knowledge of military surgery and completing his doctoral dissertation at the Imperial Military Medical Academy, which he successfully defended in 1906. Anna Nikolaevna may also have been too distracted to become involved in the revolutionary events, for she gave birth to a second daughter, Lyudmila, in July 1906.

When his year of study in St. Petersburg drew to a close, Evgeny Vladimirovich received a new appointment to the remote Aksha District on the border with Mongolia, populated by Cossacks, convicts, and Buryats.[2] Its chief town was Aksha, founded in 1765, with a population of about sixteen hundred. Three Decembrists had been exiled there after 1825. The sole doctor had resigned a year before the Beks' arrival, leaving the district with only semi-trained medical assistants to provide primary medical care. Arriving at the ridge above Aksha, Anna Nikolaevna was dismayed at the prospect, and wondered what sort of intellectual life she would find in this out-of-the-way place. With whom would she talk and debate current issues? Anna Nikolaevna was justly concerned. Traditionally the Russian intelligentsia was small but vibrant, a hothouse of ideas and plans for a just society, for the good of the people. In Aksha the number of educated people was small indeed. The local intelligentsia consisted of the teacher, often given to drink; the veterinarian, an aspiring actor; and the local authorities—the judge, the Cossack chieftain, or *ataman*, and the land captain. By good fortune all supported what became Anna Nikolaevna's pet project—the establishment of a "people's house" (*narodnyi dom*), a kind of community center such as she had known in Nerchinsk Zavod.[3]

Such community centers were still new in Russia's provinces in the early twentieth century. In the eyes of a suspicious government they posed a great potential danger of subversion. People met there to read, hear lectures, and attend plays. Classes were held for illiterate adults, where progressive teachers often encouraged workers to learn about their history and contemporary affairs, even to identify their social and political needs and potential allies. Anna Nikolaevna was fully within the traditional role of the exiled intellectual as she spearheaded the campaign to build a people's house and to launch educational and cultural programs that would bring culture to the inhabitants of Aksha. Thus it was that, even in this backwater, new ideas were fostered by the tsar's enemies as well as by his progressive civic officials.

MEMOIRS

A Year in Nerchinsk Zavod

While still on the road [into exile from St. Petersburg] I decided that I would carry out practical studies in medicine in Nerchinsk Zavod, attending in the mining department's hospital. The head of the hospital was Doctor Podtyagin, whom I had known before. I counted on his help, although I knew that, as a doctor, he did not enjoy particular confidence from the population. Having begun to attend in the hospital I met a young military doctor, Evgeny Vladimirovich Bek, who also had been exiled from Smolensk to Eastern Siberia for "political unreliability." At first he worked in the port of Posyet[4] and then was transferred to the position of district doctor for the Transbaikal Cossack Host. The Cossacks engaged in raising cattle and in agriculture, and the military authorities evidently were not worried about their reliability. Dr. Bek's reputation was excellent among the inhabitants of Nerchinsk Zavod. They said that he was a selfless doctor, a marvelous surgeon, a sensitive, sincere person, a champion of popular education; traveling around the district, he always took an interest in its schools, donated books and money to libraries, and so on. On the other hand, the wives of the engineers I knew expressed negative opinions about him: he's some sort of wild man, awkward, he does not go out, does not play cards, he avoids the company of ladies, does not drink vodka, even turns down sweet wine. He abruptly declines invitations to any kind of banquet or evening party.

Dr. E. V. Bek was an exceptional person. The life of such people merits public attention. It is my task to set forth truthfully everything that I knew of him from others and what I myself experienced with him during our fifteen years of living together.

Evgeny Vladimirovich was born in Petersburg in 1865. His father worked in the postal service, where the pay was low. There were nine children in the family (six sons and three daughters). Living was hard. The father earned additional money by giving private lessons in the evening. The older sons, including Evgeny, studied in a gymnasium, earning money as tutors. The mother, energetic, affable, and self-sacrificing, bore all the work of serving the large family on her shoulders. The daughters were younger than the sons. The father was a great music lover; he made all his sons learn one or another musical instrument and organized a home orchestra. One of the father's oddities was an aversion to smartly dressed women. If he knew that ladies were coming to see his wife, he went out ahead of time.

Evgeny Vladimirovich recounted, as a characteristic curiosity, that once elegant guests took [his father] unawares. They were already in the hall and there was no other exit from the room for him. His unwillingness to meet them was so great that he got under the bed and lay there until his wife could think of a pretext to use to get the women out of the room. His father handed this character trait on to Evgeny in a different form. He hated intensely the petty bourgeois [*meshchanskii*] cast of mind: its narrow worldview, the absence of community and scientific interests, the striving to shine in attire, furniture, and so on. In his own family he was irritated when he saw his sisters' great interest in clothes and the absence of any serious inquisitiveness. His sister, Elizaveta Vladimirovna, recounted how once he took it into his head to teach his sisters to interest themselves in nature, and so he brought them to the woods beyond town. The day was hot, and the girls were tired from the unaccustomed walk and from the heat. All their brother's efforts notwithstanding, he could not get his sisters interested in nature. Because of his direct methods of battling with petty bourgeois values he often had conflicts with his brothers and sisters.

Evgeny finished the gymnasium thanks to a stipend provided by a private individual who gave the director money to pay tuition for the best of the needy students. After he finished the gymnasium Evgeny Vladimirovich was accepted into the Military Medical Academy. Among the students Evgeny received the nickname "the ascetic" because he did not take part in binges and other types of dissolute behavior among the young. The biographies of outstanding social activists with high moral views drew his attention. In the medical world such a person was the famous N. I. Pirogov. Democratic and revolutionarily inclined doctors united then in the Pirogov Society. Evgeny Bek became a member of the Pirogov Society.[5] As a student Bek's devotion to science was so great that he selflessly offered himself as a subject for one professor's experiments. This professor was studying the influence of prolonged starvation on a person's organism. Following the assignment set by the professor Evgeny Vladimirovich subjected himself to weeks of either fasting or doing without water. This weakened his health for a long time. When Evgeny Vladimirovich was in the second-to-last year, an epidemic of cholera arose in Ufa in the summer. He went there voluntarily. At the end of the epidemic he was presented a silver charm with the inscription: "From the grateful population of the town of Ufa for help during the time of the cholera epidemic."

In 1893, after finishing the Military Medical Academy, Evgeny Vladimiro-vich was appointed junior physician of the Narvsky infantry regiment in Smolensk. For the year and a half that he served there Evgeny Vladimirovich always supported the soldiers' interests. Because of this Evgeny Vladimirovich came into conflict with the military commandant and received the order: "Leave for Port Posyet in twenty-four hours." His request to be allowed to say good-bye to his family in Petersburg was not granted. He made the journey from Odessa to the port of Posyet by sea. He described his vivid impressions during his trip in letters to his relatives. His tender love for his mother and his brothers and sisters, love he had not revealed in personal contact, also shone through in them. In 1896 he was sent to Transbaikal. From 1899 through 1903 he carried out the duties of district doctor for the Fourth Department of the Transbaikal Cossack Host with his official residence in Nerchinsk Zavod. My father lived in Nerchinsk Zavod at that time, and my personal acquaintance with Dr. Evgeny Vladimirovich Bek began there.

I met Dr. Bek for the first time in outpatient reception at the hospital. Finding out that I was a student and was coming for practical experience he came up to me straightaway, sternly, businesslike. "Here is a patient who fell from a horse and hurt his arm. Determine what is wrong with him." The picture was clear; I diagnosed a dislocation of the shoulder joint. "Set it," he ordered. I was lost as I had never done any setting. With his help the dislocation was set. "Now tell me, what is the matter with that woman's eyes? Why do you think that it is trachoma? How will you treat her?" I felt as though I were at an exam. That's the way work went every time he came to the hospital. At home I had to study the textbooks. At the same time I was pleased that he provided lots of knowledge and practical skills. Subsequently he began to give me small operations to do. When we finished office hours, conversation began. I told him about Petersburg life. He acquainted me with the data of his scientific research on a local illness unknown in medicine.[6] This interested me tremendously. Soon he began to come by in the evenings to call on me at home. Our commonality of interests and aspirations led to the growth of friendly relations between us. I will write separately in more detail about our growing closer. Until then he had lived like a hermit. His need for friendship and love blazed, and our friendship changed into mutual love. I was already thirty and he thirty-four.[7] The past was poor in romantic episodes for us both. For him and for me it was the first serious love, based on profound respect for the individual.

I lived with Father in our old house. Despite ours being a family with many children, no one remained home with Father. He lived alone. The cook was a young woman whom he later married. From his previous household Father had the horse Sivka. Previously he had been a well-known walking horse, and Father raced him. Now the horse was thirty years old and only carried water from the Altach River. Father kept a homeless lad as coachman—an orphan local people considered feeble-minded, calling him

Fig. 3.1. Dr. Evgeny Vladimirovich Bek, 1899.

"Cross-eyed Mishka." Father called him Mikhailo. According to the boy, he had lost one eye in childhood and, because the other was crossed, Mikhailo always held his head to one side. Be that as it may, the horse, the coachman, and a small cart made little trips possible. My trip with Dr. Bek and Gornyi Zerentui come vividly to mind.

I had become acquainted with Dr. Bek at the hospital, but by this time he already had started courting me evenings in my home, sometimes bringing a new book to show me that he had received in the mail, sometimes showing me material on the disease he was studying. One day I said to him that the following day I wanted to go seven versts[8] to Gornyi Zerentui to visit my older sister, Tatyana Nikolaevna. Her husband, Nikolai Fedorovich Bystrov, a mining engineer, had been appointed manager of the mine, and they had recently moved to Gornyi Zerentui. Evgeny Vladimirovich said that he also had to see the manager on business about food for patients who had been sent to him from the mine for operations. We arranged a departure time. The next day he came at the appointed time. By that time Mikhailo had already harnessed Sivka to Father's cart, which though old was reasonably intact. Mikhailo solemnly led Sivka from the gate to the front porch by his bridle. It must have been that he was afraid to brush against the gate. When we came out to take our seats Mikhailo was already sitting on the coach box. Evgeny Vladimirovich mounted quickly. When I had one foot in the cart, Mikhailo turned to me: "*Baryshnia,*[9] give me the whip." It turned out that the whip lay on the ground on my side. I had to climb down and give it to him. This little incident made us laugh and, laughing, we set out on our journey.

Our house stood on the outskirts, and the road passed between green bushes. The weather was gorgeous, and many colored butterflies flew about. Evgeny Vladimirovich was in a white military dress jacket. I do not remember my outfit. I always dressed simply, like a student. We were both in good moods; even the squeaking of the cart's un-oiled wheels amused us. Sivka drove at the same pace as when carting water. We were not in a hurry and Mikhailo sat imperturbably, the whip under his arm. I do not have any recollection of what we talked about in the early part of the journey. The road to Gornyi Zerentui went across a high ridge. At the steepest ascent we went on foot to ease venerable Sivka's labor. I recounted how in my childhood, when I was about five or six years old, I feared this steep place. Father or my aunt was taking me from Gornyi Zerentui to Nerchinsk Zavod where my older sisters were studying. When I saw how the carriage put pressure on the shafthorse it seemed to me that we would go down head over heels, and I cried, "Mama! Mama!" Later they made fun of me as a coward. The road sloped gently from the ridge, and Sivka took us quickly down the mountain. We went past a white stone prison with a high gate and, on the foothills opposite, followed the village road to the manager's house. This is the very same house where our family lived and where I spent my childhood till I was seven years old. The Bystrovs met us joyfully. My sister had a big family—two sons, three daughters and a stepdaughter. It was noisy and happy in the house. It was a harmonious family.

The men were soon discussing business, and my sister and I went into the garden. How many memories were there! There were the little shrubs under which each of us had her dollhouse where we fixed "little meals" [*kushentsa*]. We sat a while in the summerhouse that used to seem so far from the porch; back then we counted as a hero anyone who decided to run to the summer house alone in the dark twilight and then speed back pell mell, fearing that someone would grab him from behind. The entire garden, which used to seem enormous to us, now looked small.

When we returned to the house it was apparent that the men had long ago finished their business conversation. Nikolai Fedorovich loved music and literature. When we went in he was saying something about literature and mentioned Shakespeare. After dinner and tea with homemade jam and cheese tarts we hurried to start back.

On the way back Evgeny Vladimirovich, apparently influenced by his conversation with Bystrov, spoke about Shakespeare, saying, "I feel sorry for King Lear when you read how he suffered in his old age, wandering like a beggar."

I sharply replied: "I don't feel the least sorry for King Lear. All his life he enjoyed every blessing in the world, and what did he do that was good for the people? It's all right that in his old age he learned how the poor live."

Evgeny Vladimirovich was silent, evidently surprised by my harsh judgment. I thought about how he, even though exiled to Siberia as politically unreliable, had probably as vague an idea of social revolution as I had had before joining the underground Marxist circle. I wanted to acquaint him with what I had learned about Marxism in the studies of the circle. In order to start the conversation somehow, I asked whether he would do some kind of community work in addition to medicine. He said uncertainly: "I am thinking of organizing a society among schoolchildren to protect birds' nests." I exclaimed mockingly, "What a social task! At this time, when the revolution is ripening, when workers' strikes and student walkouts are going on, you are thinking about birds' nests." And I began to talk about Marx's teachings, which excite and thrill students; I talked about the capitalists' exploitation of workers, about class struggle, about the communism that I knew about. I spoke heatedly but probably skipped unsystematically from one topic to another. I was sure that he, like every decent person, had to regard Marxism with delight. I was perplexed that Evgeny Vladimirovich was silent and did not encourage me with any kind of questions. I wanted to provoke him into conversation. But we had already arrived. Sivka ran home quickly, and it was too bad that we were already stopping at our house. I began to think that Evgeny Vladimirovich was angry with me because I had made fun of his society to protect birds' nests. But he gave my hand a friendly squeeze in bidding me good-bye. I had earlier noticed that he had this good trait: he easily admitted his mistakes and did not try to hide it if he did not know something.

Before he left he said that the next day he would be leaving to tour his district for a long while. It was too bad that I would not have a chance to talk to him. When he had left I thought about him a lot, especially in relation to his cold attitude toward Marxism. Taking into consideration all that I knew about Dr. Bek I understood that he was an advocate of direct action. In Nerchinsk Zavod there were neither factories nor manufacturing plants [zavodov]. Only the name and the mineshafts scattered around the mountain reminded one that once there had been a factory here. The Cossacks among whom Dr. Bek worked were in a privileged position compared to peasants. They lived in little settlements where there was no noticeable stratification into rich and poor. In the big settlements, it's true, there were kulaks—merchants and rich cattlemen—but what could one lone revolutionary do there? The only evil that hindered even medical work was the people's darkness,[10] superstitions, and almost universal illiteracy. Dr. Bek directed his efforts to this issue. In conversations and at meetings he fought for the opening of schools, and in the big settlements where there were schools he organized libraries and distributed literature with a progressive bent. Even the society he was thinking of among schoolchildren could have great educational value in developing an interest in nature and a civilized attitude toward it. And I had mocked him. What especially elevated Dr. Bek in my eyes was his scientific work. He studied a local illness that crippled the population, studying it not only to write his doctor's dissertation but so that measures would be taken to improve the health of the population, to restore their ability to work. Bek resembled that ideal person that in my young years K. F. Lukashevich had described to us in conversations within the walls of the Institute for Noble Girls. If Bek had worked among workers he would undoubtedly have become a Marxist.

After Dr. Bek's departure there was a lull at the hospital. Although Dr. Podtyagin came for office hours, he related to patients in a formal fashion and often left ahead of time, leaving office hours to me. I was interested in getting practice in the independent diagnosis of illness and prescribing treatment. Some patients, even when Dr. Podtyagin was there, left without being examined when they found out that Dr. Bek was not there. They began to get used to me as a doctor and even began to ask me to make house calls.

When there were no patients in the hospital the pharmacist, Edmund Flormanovich Strzhalkovsky, would come find me to talk. He lived at the hospital. The door to his room opened into the same tiny corridor as the doors to the reception and operating rooms. He was a middle-aged man, very lively and sociable. He had a little pointed beard, a thin, sharp nose, and wore pince-nez. I heard comments about him like those about Gogol's Dobchinsky: he was very curious and always tried to be the first to find out any news and spread it about. Evil tongues simply called him a gossip.[11] He was not a bad conversationalist; he loved to recount various events in his life and various often improbable stories.

That is how time passed in Dr. Bek's absence. About three weeks went by.

One evening I was sitting at the desk in my corner room not far from an open window, reading a book by the light of a kerosene lamp. Suddenly my heart skipped a beat, I raised my head and that very second heard the distant sound of bells. They came closer and closer, and then suddenly became silent. This was undoubtedly the arrival of Dr. Bek. He was renting a room at the Kolotovkins, not far from our house. It was nice that he had arrived. At the same time I was surprised at myself. Why had my heart skipped a beat before I had consciously heard the sound of the bells? How could this have happened? This remained a puzzle to me.

With Dr. Bek's arrival work picked up again at the hospital. He started coming more often to see me in the evenings. For his scientific work he not only had to keep up with the Russian medical literature but also the foreign medical literature. I was very interested in the study of this illness [Osteoarthritis deformans endemica] and asked him to bring me literature to translate. He ordered French and German books on bone diseases. I knew scientific French well, since I had studied in France for two years. I read him French articles in Russian right away. Neither of us knew German so well and read with a dictionary. Reading alternated with music. He loved Tchaikovsky's "Autumn Song" and arias from the opera *Carmen*. I played the piano for him of whatever I had the music for. In the hospital we both rejoiced at successful operations and worried if there was any kind of complication. All this brought me close to him and linked me with him. Therefore I was not surprised when, after six months of friendship, he asked me to marry him.

This is what happened. When the last patient had left the operating room Evgeny Vladimirovich first cleaned up the instruments and then walked up to me and, for the first time addressing me as "thou," said, "Anichka, I love you, let's get married."[12] I answered silently with a look, and we kissed. At that moment the door was suddenly flung open and the crafty physiognomy of the pharmacist appeared. "I thought the window slammed," he fibbed. Undoubtedly he was spying on us through the crack in the door. We were embarrassed at first, like guilty schoolchildren, but that quickly passed. We had nothing to hide. The pharmacist congratulated us with a beaming face and offered to photograph us. He immediately brought his camera and took Evgeny Vladimirovich and me in our white gowns. I still have this photograph but it has faded slightly with time.

Thus in a few words our declaration of love, as they say, took place.

Returning home I found Alexander Afanasevich Savinsky (my uncle on my mother's side) at Father's. It was opportune. Father, of course, had guessed what my friendship with Dr. Bek would lead to and had gathered information about him in advance. When he heard my news, Father said, "The department ataman thinks badly of Bek." My uncle objected; "Well, why do you listen to the ataman? Go on a Sunday to the bazaar and listen to what the people say about Bek. Another man like him is nowhere to be found." Father fell silent.

After knowing each other six months we were married. There was no celebration of the wedding of any sort. The question of a wedding ceremony arose. Evgeny Vladimirovich was strongly opposed to church rituals. During my student years I had also completely renounced church religion. Bearing in mind Evgeny Vladimirovich's firm adherence to principle, I could imagine how difficult it would be for him to subject himself to walking with a crown on his head and to other ceremonies of the ritual, and suggested we manage without a wedding ceremony. He did not want to subject me to ridicule and scorn. In those days women who were not married in the church bore a stigma.[13] Further, Evgeny Vladimirovich wanted to have children, and the stigma of illegitimate birth would fall on them [if we were not married in church]. All this made him take control of himself and move to an uncharacteristic compromise. We made no special preparations for the wedding. There was no wedding party except for the necessary two witnesses. On his side Dr. Podtyagin was the witness; on my side was my childhood friend [Tonya] Ryndina. During the whole time of the wedding Evgeny Vladimirovich's dispirited mood was striking. I saw how he pressed his lips together squeamishly when the priest brought him the cup of wine. Not insisting, the priest hurried to pass the cup to me.

On leaving the church his first words to me were: "Now we are together for our entire lives." Obviously he had lightened his unpleasant state with this thought during the ceremonies. In an hour we were already off on his regular tour around the district. On his travels Evgeny Vladimirovich always brought along two boxes: in one were working medications and in the other popular literature. There were brochures published by the Pirogov Society and inexpensive publications of the classics: Tolstoy, Korolenko, Gorky, and others.[14] On the basis of his experience Evgeny Vladimirovich never distributed them for free. He knew that if a Cossack paid even three kopecks he would read the purchased book but he would simply use a book received as a gift to roll cigarettes.

While touring the district we received patients in each settlement. Evgeny Vladimirovich did not like to treat women's illnesses, and women shied away from a male doctor; therefore we received patients separately. I saw the women behind a partition, and Evgeny Vladimirovich saw the men. During breaks we handed out literature of a progressive character.

During the second tour when it was already nearly spring, we conducted an inspection of all the inhabitants of eleven settlements located where the endemic bone disease [that Dr. Bek was studying] was most prevalent. We noted down all the data on specially prepared forms. I had a camera and took pictures of the most typical cases. There were no suitable places in the houses or their cellars to develop the plates. I had to get under a table. Evgeny Vladimirovich draped all sides with blankets and I developed [the plates] by the light of a red paper lantern with a stearin candle. To dry the plates quickly I had to use the stove. Sometimes the cockroaches ate successful negatives during the night. In spite of that there were enough effective pictures.

In May [of 1902] the term of my exile from Petersburg expired. I went [to St. Petersburg] to take the exams to advance to the last year. Before my departure Evgeny Vladimirovich succeeded in tracking down evidence in the archives that brigade doctor Kashin had studied the disease along the river Urov at the beginning of the 1850s[15] and that his data had been published in a medical journal (without the year being given). Having passed the exams I busied myself searching for Kashin's article in the state library in Petersburg. I succeeded in finding the article, but in it Doctor Kashin did not distinguish that suffering as a particular disease; rather, he attributed changes in the bones to the symptoms of syphilis or malaria. In any case, these data, which I painstakingly copied down, were valuable for Dr. Bek's work.

More than thirty years have passed since the day of Dr. E. V. Bek's death; but he is still remembered by the population of those regions of Transbaikal where he happened to live and work. He lived under tsarism. As a doctor he always was sick at heart at the sight of the darkness and suffering of the people, and he strove to help, giving not only medical assistance but also fighting for enlightenment. All who knew Evgeny Vladimirovich regarded him with deep respect and love. From 1899 to 1912 he worked as a doctor with the Transbaikal Cossack Host. In 1903, when he left the Fourth Department of the Transbaikal Cossack Host, the Cossack Varlamov, who had progressive leanings, brought him a testimonial with many signatures from the inhabitants of Argunsk Station. This testimonial expressed regret over the departure of the beloved doctor in simple, sincere words, calling him the "doctor of our souls." When he left Aksha in 1912 after six years' work in the Aksha District, the inhabitants touchingly expressed their feelings in a testimonial they presented him, where they said, "the memory of you, of your work in which you cared only about the good of your fellow human beings, this memory will stay with us all our lives."

Dr. Bek is remembered in the scientific world thanks to his work in studying a particular disease, unknown until then and widespread in Transbaikal among the residents along the river Urov and along other tributaries of the Argun River.[16] Dr. Bek set forth the results of his research in the form of a dissertation, published and defended by him in Petersburg at the Military Medical Academy. In the Great Soviet Medical Encyclopedia published in 1930, there is an article with the heading "Bek's Disease"! Using E. V. Bek's data this article describes the chronic malady that manifests itself in deformities of bones at the joints or limits the mobility in the joints of arms and legs. Often beginning in school-age children, this disease gradually reduces the work capacity of the population and in extreme cases leads to complete disability. E. V. Bek did more than study the disease and describe it: at the same time he sounded the alarm, suffering from the thought that every year the number of maimed persons increases and they are given no help. He sent reports to the provincial and central administrations pointing out the need for urgent measures to study the causes of the disease and appropriate measures to combat it. But the administration during the tsar's regime was indifferent to the sufferings of the people. On one of the reports the governor of Chita had written a remarkable resolution: "Transfer sick Cossacks into the peasant class."[17] During business trips to Petersburg Evgeny Vladimirovich managed to obtain the delivery of six patients to Petersburg for clinical study at government cost. But such a study could do nothing to explain the causes of the disease, which were rooted in some sort of local conditions. Dr. Bek gave lectures to different scientific organizations (of doctors, geologists, and chemists), showing the patients. This evoked great interest in the disease. After the lectures, resolutions were passed in all the societies: "Organize a spring expedition to the heart of the illness." But there were no funds for it.

Only under Soviet power did the work that Dr. Bek started receive broad scope. Large funds were released for the opening of a special scientific research station. Every year they organized expeditions, improved the water supply, and had the sick treated at Yamkun health resort.

How enthusiastic Dr. Bek would have been to work under the new conditions, if only his life had not been abruptly cut short, through the fault of the tsarist administration!

The Russo-Japanese War

In 1903 Evgeny Vladimirovich was sent to Petersburg to update his surgical skills. Before this I had left for Petersburg to take the fifth-year course in the Medical Institute. In 1903 I received the diploma of doctor with distinction. When the Russo-Japanese War started Evgeny Vladimirovich's study trip had not yet finished. He was mobilized as a surgeon in a division field hospital for work on the front line.

Women doctors were not taken into the army at that time. I joined up as supernumerary nurse in the Twelfth Mobile Field Hospital that was supposed to work for the same division not more than seven versts[18] from the field hospital. Although I was counted as a nurse, in the hospital during the war I was entrusted as a doctor with a ward of patients.

Veresaev's book, *In the War,* wonderfully describes all the horrors of poor organization and the irresponsibility of the authorities.[19] Our Twelfth Hospital and divisional field hospital stayed a long time in Mukden with nothing to do. The head of the division, General Morozov, and his adjutants spent time enjoyably, holding picnics with nurses and doctors. Evgeny Vladimirovich and I were not a part of this.

Discovering that there were many illiterates among the soldiers serving the hospital I organized a circle and began to teach them to read. It turned out that this attracted the authorities' distrust of me, although I was unaware of it. There already had been an outburst against me when our army made its great and disorderly retreat after the battle at Vafangou [*sic*].[20] One of the soldiers from the hospital, weakened by a chronic intestinal catarrh, could not walk and sat down in an empty two-wheeled cart. A bursar struck him so hard that a wound appeared on his cheek and blood ran from his ear. I bandaged him. After supper, when all the doctors got together, I asked the head of the hospital whether he knew that the bursar had drawn a soldier's blood. He did not answer. Indignant at the silence, I asked, "Does the soldier have a right to complain?" The head of the hospital leapt up and in an enraged voice cried, "If you don't like how we do things here you can just get out!"

In the morning they gave me a two-wheeled cart and, gathering my things, I went to find the divisional field hospital. With the army in flight everything was mixed up. I first tracked down the staff headquarters—with difficulty— but they knew absolutely nothing about the whereabouts of the different sectors. At the same time I was flabbergasted: in this general chaos, at the moment of my appearance, the entire headquarters personnel were getting ready to be photographed. The chief of staff sat in the center, with his dog, with the others around him.

Finally, from a chance meeting with a soldier, I learned that the divisional field hospital was in Gunzhulin.[21] Getting there, I met Evgeny Vladimirovich. He advised me to write down all the circumstances of my expulsion from the hospital and to send it as a letter to the newspaper *Russian Physician*.[22] I did so, and my letter was published. In response, this same *Russian Physician* printed a letter from all the doctors of the hospital. In it they vindicated the chief doctor and, noting their generally good attitude toward me as a doctor, charged me with tactlessness, because I had asked: "Does a soldier have the right to complain?" in the presence of the officers' servants. In Veresaev's book, *In the War*, in the first edition, this whole incident is described, using the real names, in the chapter "Who Stood at the Bedside of the Sick Soldier?" Veresaev was especially indignant about the doctors' response to my letter. In later editions of *In the War* the account of this incident was eliminated by the censor.[23] I was soon invited to serve as doctor in the mobile Red Cross hospital where I worked till the end of the war.

Recollections of Life in Aksha

After the conclusion of the Russo-Japanese War we returned to Petersburg where Evgeny Vladimirovich had been sent before the war to update his surgical skills. His dissertation on the topic "An Endemic Bone-Joint Disease in Transbaikal" attracted great scientific interest. The military department brought in six Cossacks with various degrees of skeletal deformation. They were further studied in different clinics in Petersburg. In spite of Evgeny Vladimirovich's service in medical research and practice, at the end of his study tour he was again appointed district doctor to the Transbaikal Cossack Host in an even more distant and remote region, bordering a sparsely populated part of Mongolia. Evidently his reputation as "politically unreliable" was decisive. The town of Aksha was to serve as our residence. We left for Aksha in the middle of September 1906. Two months before our departure I gave birth to a daughter and we had to make the distant journey with a newborn baby. We traveled as far as Chita by rail, but 220 versts

Fig. 3.2. Photograph of the town of Aksha, Transbaikal, taken by Anna Bek on her arrival there in 1906.

farther on horseback along the stony Akshinsk road.[24] We rode on horse-back for three days in freezing weather. Deep snow lay in the fields, cover-ing the still unharvested grain. The backwardness of the population in this region could be seen in the fact that remnants of the ancient pre-Christian religion were still preserved here. At the postal station an old woman told us: "The reason the snow covered the grain in the fields is that people have stopped honoring the god Perun."[25] On the last crossing, when we ascended a steep ridge, the cheerless view of the town of Aksha opened before us. Situated on the banks of the Onon River, Aksha looked like a mid-sized village; gray huts [*izbushki*] were visible, with large vegetable gardens, and there was a church on the square in the center. This view gave us uncom-fortable pause. "What kind of life awaits us in this out-of-the-way place!"

We found an apartment of three small rooms in the home of a merchant who had died. Taking a look about town we learned that it had a hospital, the biggest wooden building, and that there were two merchants' houses with shops, also distinguished by their size. The three-year parish school found shelter in a little tiny house.

We first became acquainted with the teacher. He told us that life in Aksha passed boringly, monotonously. On holidays there were drunkenness and fighting. He showed us a letter from one of his older pupils (which had somehow fallen into his hands). The pupil wrote to his friend in Chita: "St. Peter's Day here was fun. Uncle Kuzma got his eyes knocked out in a fight, and Petrukha got sloshed and broke his leg." Holiday conversations, according to the teacher, were enlivened only by gossip. Most often the subject of the gossip was the wife of the senior doctor of the hospital who, trying to look younger than her age, allowed herself various liberties, perhaps out of boredom. Recently, at a crowded name-day party for a merchant, she first sat on the lap of one man and then suddenly bestowed a kiss on another. The population of the town was divided into Cossacks and petty bourgeois traders and artisans [meshchane]. Relations between them were hostile. The great majority of the population of Aksha was illiterate. We learned later that the teacher himself often got drunk and that many times he even showed up drunk at lessons.

The intelligentsia in Aksha consisted of the judge, the hospital doctor, the veterinarian, the ataman of the Second Cossack Department, and the land captain.[26] In the course of the first year, Evgeny Vladimirovich was completely engulfed in his doctor's work. Traveling about the stations of his district he found many patients needing surgical help. He submitted a petition to add a special operating room onto the hospital. He succeeded in this. From his first year as the doctor, Evgeny Vladimirovich won the confidence and love of the people. He approached every patient attentively, thoughtfully, prescribing treatment without ever resorting to the routine writing out of prescriptions. Faith in him especially grew when he enabled two long blind persons to see through cataract operations. He saw one of them driving down the street. You often heard: "We never laid eyes on such a doctor!"

Since I was occupied with my infant in arms, I did not have a job. I set myself the goal of opening a Sunday school for illiterates. I was able to open the school in the small quarters of the parish school. At first only ten adolescents signed up. Adults did not come to study. The wife of the veterinarian, a former teacher, helped me to organize the school. Her husband, P. M. Didenko, turned out to be a great lover of theater arts. He and I began to think about the possibility of organizing a drama circle. Among the young people there were enough wanting to participate in a drama circle, but there was no place to put on plays. Whether we were discussing organizing public readings or a library, we kept coming up with the idea of building a community center [narodnyi dom]. The town had no funds for this; we would have to find the money. At Evgeny Vladimirovich's suggestion, the town elder drew up a subscription list. Evgeny Vladimirovich took up collecting money energetically. As the district doctor he never took honoraria offered for treatment, not only from poor Cossacks but also from rich ones.[27] In many stations in Evgeny Vladimirovich's district there were rich men, cattle breeders, who counted their stock by the hundred and even by the thousand. With their big families they often turned to Evgeny Vladimirovich for medical help. Instead of an honorarium, Evgeny Vladimirovich offered them the subscription list for the community center and they donated generously. Evgeny Vladimirovich sent me the Cossack women with women's illnesses and I, as the stand-in for the district doctor, also offered the subscription list in place of an honorarium. Merchants donated overdue promissory notes. We took them and, from the more well-to-do [debtors], received fairly large sums on these notes through the court. We organized a lottery and in these ways collected enough money to build the community center. The Aksha population showed its support by transporting the logs [for construction] for free.

The festive opening of the community center took place in the third year of our life in Aksha. The drama circle was organized by that time, and Ostrovsky's play, "Poverty Is Not a Vice," was prepared for presentation.[28] The play went very successfully. The shortcomings in the acting of the young, local actors were concealed by the artistic acting of the veterinarian who played the role of Lyubim Tortsov; he won the audience's heart with his acting. Watching his acting, you could not help but wonder: "Why is he wasting his life as an ordinary veterinarian when he could be an outstanding artist on any great stage?" After the play there were dances to the music of local balalaika players.

The opening of the community center allowed us to hold public readings and to organize a library and a local museum. At Evgeny Vladimirovich's initiative we had begun to collect exhibits for the museum in our apartment from our first year of living in Aksha. A prehistoric human site turned up in a sandy valley not far from the town. With the help of schoolchildren we dug up arrowheads, pottery shards, and other things. Gold prospectors, knowing of our mission to create a local museum, brought us rare minerals. Beautiful amethyst crystals, rock crystal, and other minerals turned up in the mountains near Aksha. Local hunters brought various kinds of birds and wild animals. With the help of an instruction book we learned to stuff animals. One of the local girls, Utyuzhnikova, who attended the Sunday school, helped us in this with particular skill. All these exhibits filled our apartment until the opening of the community center.

Our enemy in Aksha turned out to be the local priest. As someone informed us, he wrote to Chita denouncing us, pointing out that we did not attend church and distracted the attention of young parishioners by holding rehearsals on Saturdays. As a result, on orders from Chita, two representatives of the local police turned up at our apartment with a search warrant. Evgeny Vladimirovich was on tour fighting plague in the district, and I had to receive them. Both looked embarrassed. They began by apologizing for disturbing me, showed me the order, and proceeded to search. Their task of finding illegal literature in our house presented them with great difficulty. We had lots of books. When we arrived in Aksha, greatly inflated talk about us said that we brought forty puds of books.[29] One of our rooms looked like a library. Two walls were completely filled with books on simple wooden shelves. The greatest number of books and journals were on medical subjects, followed by psychological and pedagogical literature and belles lettres. I had been interested in psychology from my student years. Marxism gave me the impetus to study the development of the psyche [*dushu v razvitii*], both in connection with the physiology of the brain and under the influence of the environment, to which the famous experiments of Pavlov and Bekhterev led.[30] In Aksha at that time I read Ushinsky's book, *Man as the Object of Education,* with enthusiasm.[31] To investigate all the books and to evaluate them from a political point of view was a job beyond the powers of the representatives of the police, who did not even have a secondary education. They pondered [words in] the book titles: "pediatrics," "ophthalmology," and others. I had to explain the contents of each book to them. Turning a few books over in their hands, they preferred to believe my words that we did not have any illegal literature, and they withdrew, once again excusing themselves for disturbing me. And that's how the affair of the denunciation ended.[32]

It is interesting that even the land captain was sympathetic to the idea of a community center. When the construction was just finishing up we got the news that the governor was making a tour through all the sectors of the Transbaikal Cossack Host and would travel through Aksha. We were worried because the biggest building, under construction in the center of the town, would certainly attract the governor's attention, and he could forbid the opening of a community center. Indeed, when the governor arrived, he asked, "What is that building being built there?" The land captain who was escorting him answered, "That is a public building for the school and town office." Thus the storm passed.

After the community center opened the most active individuals opened a society for the community center. Its members were supposed to look after all its needs and develop cultural-educational work. From the very first it was decided to plant a garden around the house. Schoolchildren were drawn in to plant trees. The veterinarian's wife, Alevtina Aleksandrovna Didenko, organized a children's choir and a drama circle among the schoolchildren. We prepared a play for adults or a popular reading with a magic lantern or a children's play for every holiday. I did not act in the plays myself, although sometimes I wanted to take a suitable role, remembering my earlier success in amateur theatricals in Nerchinsk Zavod. But here I was held back by the thought that it was important to promote local strengths. People wanting to act were always found for every role. The director was always the veterinarian, P. M. Didenko, and the prompter, the teacher. For some evening plays the teacher turned up drunk; it then fell to me to get into the prompter's box. The choice of play and rehearsal always took place with my participation. We read the play aloud and discussed it collectively beforehand. Evgeny Vladimirovich did not appear publicly himself at the community center, but his sympathy and readiness to provide assistance in everything facilitated and enlivened the work of the circle.

My medical work in Aksha was limited to seeing sick women at home. At the hospital Evgeny Vladimirovich enlisted me to assist him in the more serious operations.

Marriage and Family

In the typical, ordinary novel the basic subject is falling in love and over-coming various obstacles to entering into marriage. At the novel's happy ending it seems to the reader that from the moment of marriage the he-roes' happy life begins, unmarred by any clouds. In reality there are not many completely happy marriages. Life together demands great work on oneself: one has to change one's habits a great deal, round off sharp edges in one's own character. Formerly in marriage, according to *Domostroi*,[33] where the wife had to subordinate herself completely to her husband, such work of self-reconstruction fell exclusively on the woman. Now woman has learned to claim her rights, and mutual polishing of their characters is necessary for their peaceful life together: work on oneself, improvement, and the removal of undesirable character traits.

My marriage to Dr. E. V. Bek was, to my mind, exceptionally happy: a common worldview and interest in community and scientific work brought us all the closer after our marriage and strengthened our friendship. Nev-ertheless, even in our lives, especially in the first year of our life together, there were frictions and conflicts. Our first little conflict comes to mind particularly vividly. After the wedding we traveled in his district where I worked together with Evgeny Vladimirovich. When we returned to Nerchinsk Zavod I found out that the local drama circle was going to put on a play, "On the Threshold of the Case" [*Na poroge k delu*], at the club. Before I had left for my courses [at medical school] I sometimes took part myself in the drama circle; and after the play a dance was always held. I loved to dance. Now, accustomed to working together with Evgeny Vladimirovich, I had no doubt that we would go together to the play.

But he sharply refused to go to the club.

I tried to persuade him, begged him, I came to tears. But he stood firm. Finally I became angry; I dressed hurriedly and left for the club alone. There I saw in my acquaintances' glances that they noticed my red-rimmed eyes, but no one asked the cause. Obviously they could guess the reason without asking. The play dragged on to the end; I did not stay for the dance. On the way home I thought about our conflict, and understood that I was wrong. Evgeny Vladimirovich, for all the time he had lived in Nerchinsk Zavod, had never gone once to the club. He disapproved of card playing, did not like to dance and did not know how. In general, he had a deeply rooted negative feeling about club diversions. If he suddenly came with his wife it would look as though his wife led him, like "a bull by the nose." He was proud. It was not right for me to coax him to come with me when he had no desire to.

Arriving home I saw that he had not gone to bed, that he was waiting for me. I could see by his face that he felt guilty. I wanted to change his mood right away. I said: "You were right not to come. The play did not go too well."

Thus our first conflict ended. There were also other types of frictions and conflicts, but they were all of a short-lived nature. The basic cause of our conflicts was my overly great touchiness and his quick temper. It was enough for him to say one harsh word for me to fall into deep dejection and my tearful reaction to the offense would begin. Evgeny Vladimirovich could not bear tears, but in spite of all my efforts I could not overcome this teary reflex, which I myself hated in myself. Evgeny Vladimirovich told me: "One must make allowances. If I were phlegmatic I would think over every word before speaking. In years past, at home, if something annoyed me, I was capable of snatching a glass and smashing it to smithereens on the floor, and then I was ashamed of myself. Thus my harsh words may fly out, independent of my consciousness." This characteristic of his gave us both a stimulus—for me not to take offense, for him to control himself. Obviously we were both successful in softening the sharp edges in our character, and in later years I do not recall that we had any conflicts.

There is one more aspect of marriage that can darken life—and that is jealousy. There turned out to be no basis for jealousy in my working life with Evgeny Vladimirovich. All the same, some traces of jealousy crept in. On my side there were two such instances. After four months of our life together I went to Petersburg to take the examinations for promotion to the last year of the Medical Institute. Evgeny Vladimirovich accompanied me to Stretensk where I caught the train.[34] Before my departure he rented a room at my friend Ryndina's house. I was held up in Petersburg because the term of my exile from the capital had not fully ended and the administration of the Medical Institute did not have permission to allow me to take the exams. I received a letter from my friend. She wrote that Evgeny Vladimirovich was taking my absence very hard; in order to divert him she often went to see him when he was in. This letter provoked my jealousy. My friend was very beautiful and always dressed elegantly. I imagined that Evgeny Vladimirovich would be carried away by her, and this thought tormented me. Later, after our return to Nerchinsk Zavod, when I told Evgeny Vladimirovich about this, he said, "She isn't at all like you, I didn't even like to look at her." He always told the truth and I was reassured.

The second instance was during the Russo-Japanese War, when the whole division was in reserve and our hospitals were four kilometers from Mukden, in tents spread out on the steppe. Evgeny Vladimirovich had a separate tent; I was in a big tent together with the nurses. One time some other division's hospital pitched its tents there. Among the personnel there one nurse stood out from the others: she was pretty, shapely, very sociable, and she had a pleasant voice and sang opera arias beautifully. Involuntarily I, just like all the others, was enraptured by her. Once I saw with amazement that Evgeny Vladimirovich was talking animatedly to her, she was showing him her photographs. (Usually he avoided new people.) Another time they were again talking and I heard their last words. She was asking him to help her write some kind of application. He told her: "Come to my tent tomorrow morning." I felt pangs of jealousy. "Tomorrow they'll spend a long time writing some application and Evgeny Vladimirovich will be fascinated by her beauty." This thought troubled me all night; in the morning I purposely went to the side of that hospital's tents and met her. "What was the matter with her? Why was there a big bandage on her cheek?" Coming closer I saw how her face was disfigured. During the night she had had an abscess, her cheek had swollen so much that even her nose was lopsided. Jealousy is a nasty feeling—it always makes one happy at the misfortunes of a rival. I was pleased with this temporary disappearance of the beauty of her face and calmly watched how the nurse went into Evgeny Vladimirovich's tent. In a day that hospital moved somewhere else.

About the same time I saw that Evgeny Vladimirovich was also capable of being jealous. In the division infirmary there was another doctor, Chernyavsky, with whom Evgeny Vladimirovich had good relations. This doctor was interested in psychology and philosophy. Sometimes he came up to me to talk about abstract topics. Each time I noticed that no sooner had Chernyavsky come up to me than Evgeny Vladimirovich's mood changed for the worse: he became sullen, irritable. Once, after a sultry day, Evgeny Vladimirovich suggested that we go for a walk on the steppe in the evening. After we started out, Chernyavsky came up unobserved and walked along next to me. Suddenly Evgeny Vladimirovich sharply said, almost shouted: "What are you here for?" Chernyavsky recoiled at once and went back.

These little facts did not disturb Evgeny Vladimirovich's and my relationship, they were like fleeting clouds, because they had no serious basis. But in many cases jealousy, like a dark storm cloud, ruins family life that otherwise, it would seem, could have been happy.

[In Aksha] there were no conflicts of any kind in our family. Coming home tired after work, Evgeny Vladimirovich loved to play a little with our daughter. When he left on long trips he always took a photograph of our daughter and me with him so that he would not feel lonely, he said. His return from the trip was a joyous holiday for us; taking me and our daughter by the hand he loved to whirl around the room with us repeating in a sing-song voice: "We are together again! We are together again!"

When our daughter reached six years of age we began to think that it was coming time to begin her education, but in Aksha there was no gymnasium. At that time Evgeny Vladimirovich was invited to take the job of medical inspector for the mining district, with his residence in Chita. He decided to take the offer, although we were sorry to leave what was going so well in Aksha.

On the day of our departure, when everything was already packed up and the troika of horses stood at the porch, delegations from the inhabitants of Aksha and the town government appeared unexpectedly at our house carrying testimonials. The leave-taking was from the heart. After our departure the town submitted a petition to award Evgeny Vladimirovich and me the title of hereditary honorary citizen of Aksha. Governor Kiyashko turned down the petition, justifying this by citing our political unreliability.[35]

4.

Making a Career: Chita in War and Revolution

Anna Nikolaevna moved to the city of Chita in 1912, and left it in 1923 with much regret. Here she lived happily with her husband, developed her career in education and public service, became the major financial and emotional support of her family, and began her professional presentations and writing. These were years in which she learned much about herself and what she could do.

Capital of the Transbaikal, Chita was a relatively developed city of more than fifty thousand when she moved there.[1] It boasted more than twenty schools, twelve churches, including an Orthodox cathedral, a Roman Catholic church, a Jewish synagogue, a mosque, and a convent. Its civic institutions included several charitable organizations helping orphans, students, immigrants, and the families of convicts; museums and a branch of the Imperial Geographic Society; professional organizations of teachers and doctors; and literary, singing, and drama circles. Located on the Chita and Ingoda rivers, the city was an important railroad junction of the Trans-Siberian Railroad and an important track south to the Chinese border. There were factories and trading firms, banks and insurance firms, and two hotels. While there was a small intelligentsia connected to the city's professions, schools, and newspapers, wealthy merchants dominated the town, some of whom maintained grand homes with ballrooms, libraries, and greenhouses. The Beks' new house was also large and comfortable, with electricity, a telephone, and another wonderful luxury for those days, indoor plumbing.

Then, as today, the city was the center of an important military border district, and was the headquarters of the Second Siberian Army Corps of the Imperial Army. A significant segment of the population was military, and soldiers were a common sight in the city. Another significant minority was the Chinese population, who had come across the nearby border to trade and had settled in. There were little Chinese stands on the street corners and, in a Chinese section of the city, shops with gorgeous silks and brocades as well as tiny shoes that were still being sold to women with bound feet. Chinese carried baskets of snowy laundry home to their owners, or little shoe cleaning and repair kits to fix the shoes of passersby. Others sold fresh vegetables that they grew on the outskirts of town.

A tragic accident forced Anna Nikolaevna into new independence and maturity. In 1915 her husband died from complications of typhus that he had caught while caring for Turkish prisoners of war. Suddenly she became the family's chief provider and head of the household. Although she was grief-stricken at her beloved husband's death, there is no hint in the memoirs that

Fig. 4.1. The Beks' house in Chita.

her new responsibilities unnerved her; rather, she seems to have continued her way of life with aplomb and energy. This may be explained by the sort of marriage she and Evgeny Vladimirovich had. He was often away from home, traveling about his district or staying very late in the hospital except on Sundays. Anna Nikolaevna was very much on her own, busy in her medical practice and teaching career. She was accustomed to making independent decisions in her work and in the public organizations that she served. Anna Nikolaevna wrote about her husband with more respect than passion, but that is consistent with the genre and the times. She poignantly asserts, however, that after his death she continued to feel his presence, closer in some ways now than during his life when his medical work dominated his time.

After Evgeny Vladimirovich's death, Anna Nikolaevna's house continued to be a center of social activity. One of her sisters lived in Chita, and other members of the family came to stay during times of stress—her brother Nikolai's family followed him to prison in Siberia, and her brother Innokenty and his family came to live with her after fleeing famine in Petrograd in 1918. The home became the heart of family activity; the children published a daily newspaper with one uncle, and family members entertained themselves with singing, piano playing, and amateur theatricals.[2]

It is clear, however, that Anna Nikolaevna is not telling the reader anywhere near the full story about her life during these years. Where, for instance, is World War I? It is perhaps understandable that it gets short shrift; Siberians may have felt the European war to be very distant. Still, in Siberia as in the rest of the empire, men were called up to serve in the army, and women filled the jobs they left, keeping farms and factories going. Siberian industries, especially along the rail line, expanded to meet new requirements as European Russian production changed in content and destination. Siberian businessmen joined together in hitherto forbidden groups to coordinate production and transportation. In her account, however, the major impact of the war is the death of her husband, which she blames on the tsarist government.

And then the events of 1917 burst out in Russia—two revolutions within eight months of each other! First the monarchy fell in February, and then the temporary Provisional Government in Petrograd, a coalition of liberals and moderate socialists, was overthrown by the Bolshevik Party. A new Soviet communist government came to power, bringing excitement and hopes for radical change to some, horror and dread to others. When news of the tsar's abdication in early March arrived in Chita, the inhabitants accepted it calmly. Along with one of her brothers Anna Nikolaevna served on the Committee of Public Safety, elected by the populace to run the city after the fall of the tsarist government, but we know neither why she was chosen nor what she did. Although she writes nothing about any concern for women's causes or specifically women's activities, the local Women's Council nominated her to run in the national elections for the Constituent Assembly in the fall of 1917; we know one woman won a seat but not whether it was she.[3] After the Bolshevik coup in October, local Communists took charge and disbanded the committee. Despite the tumultuous changes in Chita, Anna Nikolaevna writes little about the events in her city and region, and almost nothing about the creation of a new state. Given her past in radical student politics, her Marxism and social activism, we can assume that she must have been pleased first to see the tsar overthrown and then the Bolsheviks win. She says little about the fates of the committees and councils she worked closely with in Chita, however, or about the new institutions the Bolsheviks, some of whom she knew in Chita, were creating.

Then, from 1918 to 1921, civil war raged across Russia between the Bolshevik Red Army and a broad spectrum of their opponents. In Siberia as elsewhere bands of White and Red soldiers drafted able-bodied men by force, and emptied granaries to feed themselves and their horses. They confiscated workhorses for the army and helped themselves to fowl and other food. Anna Nikolaevna says little about the war, although its impact on Siberia in general and Chita in particular was enormous. Eastern Siberia was controlled by one of the most notorious figures of the war, Grigory Semenov, a Cossack ruler with no apparent political plan save his own aggrandizement and enrichment. Chita came under his control in 1918 and became his headquarters. As he defeated one force after another and cities fell to his army, he devised a rough-and-ready rule. He largely left tsarist institutions in place but tightened controls and imprisoned or executed radicals.[4] Semenov was defeated in October 1920, however, and by the end of 1920 the Bolsheviks controlled most of Siberia, although, in some areas, Reds and Whites continued to struggle until early 1922. The Siberian economy was in ruins, and the exhausted population was decimated by typhus, typhoid, diphtheria, and local famines.

Why did Anna Nikolaevna write so little about politics, the revolution, or civil war?[5] Writing in the late Stalinist years, she undoubtedly censored her own writing and storytelling. Before writing her memoirs she had experienced bitter battles with the Communist Party, and had lost a brother in the Stalinist camps. Second, her strictly political activities were few. As she relates in this chapter, she declined to join any political party, refusing an offer to join the Bolsheviks because she would not have the party dictate to her with whom she could work or be friends. But she befriended Bolsheviks at some risk to herself, and her memoir gives the strong impression that she sympathized with the ideals and goals of the Soviet government.

In addition, Anna Nikolaevna devoted considerable time to her daughter Lyudmila, nicknamed Lyusya, despite what she says in this chapter. Having moved to Chita to put Lyusya into school, she still taught her at home for a few years. Anna Nikolaevna believed in the importance of labor education for children and insisted that Lyusya do a certain amount of housework despite the fact that a household helper was almost always living with them. To improve her Russian Lyusya had to keep a journal that her mother corrected every night. She also sent Lyusya to a neighbor's for French lessons and to swimming lessons at a nearby school. It was winter, and there was no place to swim, so the teacher had the children lie on the desks and practice the appropriate kicks and arm strokes!

Finally, this chapter reveals that her heart lay not in politics but in her career and her public activities, which continued to expand during and after the revolution. In a revealing passage she expresses amazement and dismay at the decision of the kindergarten teacher, a member of the Socialist Revolutionary Party, to abandon the poor children in her charge for politics. Anna Nikolaevna does not write about her medical practice in Chita, but local newspapers reveal that she regularly advertised that she saw private patients at home, and she served a brief stint as director of the local mental hospital. In addition to her medical practice, from the time she arrived in Chita she was busy teaching, including science courses in a girls' high school, courses she established for teachers of preschool, and Sunday schools for illiterate adults. She began her own scientific research into medical and educational problems, and gave public lectures on her findings. We learn in this chapter that she was an early follower of the progressive ideas of her renowned contemporary, the Italian doctor and educator Maria Montessori. Local newspapers reflect her unflagging interest in nonpolitical community causes: kindergartens, libraries, museums, the university in Irkutsk, and parents' and teachers' associations, and her election to such bodies as the administration of the Union of Women, the Teachers' Union, and the school committee of the town council. As Chita changed hands between Red and White forces and back again, she continued to do what she had been doing as best she could, especially in the field of adult education; this was the work she preferred, and it was those students she was most sorry to leave in 1923 when she left Chita.

Anna Nikolaevna also took jobs of short duration, summer jobs that brought her pay and took her into the countryside where food was more plentiful during the civil war years. She took in boarders and family members who helped to pay bills and care for the household and her daughter. Throughout the years of war and civil war her household lived as much as it could from its own gardens. In a further effort to supply themselves with food, Anna Nikolaevna's household bought a pig. She delivered piglets that were warmly welcomed by the children, and one can imagine the fun they had with this new family inhabiting the toilet room; but the piglets sickened and died. Another experiment in household animal husbandry turned out to be no more successful when one of her brothers bought two rabbits, expecting them to breed prolifically. To his surprise, the rabbits fought constantly and there were no babies. It turned out that both rabbits were male, and both ended up in the dinner pot.

When Anna Nikolaevna left Chita in 1923 for a faculty position at the University of Irkutsk, she was quite a different person from the one who had arrived in 1912. Like thousands of other Siberians, she had begun adapting to the new order in Communist Russia. Much was the same; the same bureaucracies with different names did the same jobs as before with many of the same values, good and bad habits, even some of the same personnel. But the ideals of the Soviet state differed radically from its tsarist predecessor, and as a public-minded physician and scientist, and supporter of progressive ideas in education, Anna Nikolaevna endorsed the social and cultural goals of the new state. She adapted to her new personal circumstances as well. As a wife she had struck out on her own path in Aksha and Chita, and now, as a widow, she was even freer to choose which interests to develop. Popular with her colleagues, she won elected positions that gave her the power to found and develop the educational institutions she cared about. She presented cogent arguments and won over bureaucracies. Her interests had clearly moved a long way from clinical medicine. Her decision to move to Irkutsk in 1923 was in part to stay close to her daughter, but it was no less to realize the potential of her now enthusiastic interest in the physiology and psychology of learning.

MEMOIRS

Recollections of Life in Chita (1912–1923)

Evgeny Vladimirovich spent the first year of life in the town of Chita traveling around the mining region, and I was busy setting up the household. According to the conditions of his service the mining administration was supposed to provide us with an apartment, but there was nothing available. Instead of an apartment they offered us a loan to build a house. It became my job to find a plot of land, make the purchase, put together a plan for the house conforming to our needs, and so on. In the same year the Chita society of teachers, knowing of my interest in popular education, elected me chairwoman of the society. The head of a private girls' gymnasium invited me to teach courses on anatomy, physiology, and psychology in the upper classes. Thus in Chita, too, I pursued a path other than clinical medicine. Through the teachers I had a link with many schools, which gave a new impetus to my interest in questions of the development of the psyche [*razvitie dush*] from the Marxist point of view. The issue of combating children's poor performances in school especially interested the teachers. I suggested they send me the unsuccessful ones to study them from as many angles as possible. Moreover, the teachers sending me children had to give their school records. As a result of this research I accumulated significant material over a number of years that I used later in 1922 for two published articles.[6]

Even earlier I had become interested in the classic work of Séguin on the education of idiots and the book by Séguin's student Montessori, *The Children's House,* where a system of educating preschoolers is set forth.[7] Together with Ushinsky's classic book, *Man as the Object of Education,*[8] this literature completely convinced me of the necessity of a labor education for the proper development of the child. This pushed me to give a public lecture on the theme, "Labor Education and the Montessori System."[9] My lecture attracted a large audience and evoked great interest in the question of the labor education of children. On several occasions after the lecture I met parents on the street with whom I was not acquainted. They stopped me and asked questions related to my talk or shared their difficulties in bringing up their own children. This was at the beginning of 1914, when life had not yet been upset by the war.

The lecture took place in the large general hall of the public assembly [building].[10] When Evgeny Vladimirovich and I arrived, the hall was crowded to overflowing; not only below but also in the balconies all the places were taken and a number [of people] were even standing. Such interest can probably be explained by the fact that a revolutionary mood was already growing in the city. The very word "labor" and "laboring" already promised something new and progressive. (Maybe Evgeny Vladimirovich's and my popularity also had something to do with it.) He (Evgeny Vladimirovich) sat in the first row. The large size of the crowd gave me particular inspiration, since I was trying to popularize as much as possible the idea of labor education (according to Ushinsky and others). I divided my lecture into two parts and, finishing the first part, took a break and went out to a nearby room. Many people rushed after me, evidently wanting to question me or share their thoughts. Evgeny Vladimirovich stood at the door and barred it; I heard him repeat to all of them, "You have to let her rest," "Let her rest." He had not known the contents of my lecture because before this he had returned from making a tour of the district as medical inspector. I saw that he was excited by the beginning of my lecture and satisfied with it. After the second part the audience's comments began. All responded enthusiastically to the lecture. Some said that such lectures were needed more often. One solid citizen said, "The lecture is our holiday today on Ussuriiskaya Street." Several people expressed the wish that a pedagogical society be organized so that educational issues could be studied in greater depth. I had had the idea of organizing a pedagogical society myself. I took advantage of these comments and settled then and there that all who were interested in organizing a pedagogical society should meet at my house. I fixed the day and time. That is how my public lecture ended.

When Evgeny Vladimirovich and I walked home, it was a freezing night, and he would not permit me to talk so that I would not get a sore throat. At home, as soon as we took off our fur coats, Evgeny Vladimirovich came up to me with a shining face, and said, "I love you, Anichka!" We kissed. This was an expression of our spiritual closeness. After that he went away into his office. We always slept in different rooms, which caused gossips to say that we were not husband and wife, that Evgeny Vladimirovich had a real wife somewhere. Our eight-year-old daughter slept next to me. She was already asleep when I came home. I could not get to sleep for a long time that night from an abundance of happiness. I was trying to apply Ushinsky's ideas of labor education to my daughter, and her development pleased me. It seemed that everything testified to our happy life and I had no premonition that misfortune was already close by, that great sorrow was awaiting me. It was winter, the beginning of 1914.

Soon after the lecture, on the appointed day, the founders of the pedagogical society met at my house. Using some model charter, we made up one for the society and addressed ourselves to the local authorities for permission [to open]. But the tsarist officials at that time were afraid of any kind of society and did not allow us to open. I then appealed in a letter to the pedagogue N. Kartsov, well known then in Petersburg, who was at that time chairman of the Petersburg parents' society. He regarded our work very sympathetically, and soon we received an official proposal to open a branch of the Petersburg society in Chita. Thus bypassing the local powers and red tape, we founded a branch in Chita under the humble name "The Parents' Circle."[11] We set as our chief task the opening of a kindergarten on the city outskirts for unsupervised children. We charged for lectures on educational questions so as to collect money for the kindergarten.

In the summer of 1914 the first imperialist war broke out. Evgeny Vladimirovich was mobilized as a surgeon for work in the Chita hospital. After several months of work in the hospital he protested more than once against misappropriation of wounded soldiers' food. The dishonest, greedy hospital administration was robbing soldiers of the value of their rations.[12]

Even those with stomach wounds and those recuperating from serious operations received neither milk nor white bread. These soldiers died from the coarse food. Evgeny Vladimirovich entered an uneven battle: he protested, he wrote reports and complaints. A menacing cloud hung over our heads. As a lone warrior on the field of battle, he could not win but he also could not reconcile himself to the soldiers' deaths. He came home depressed and became irritable. Life became cheerless.

I remember one occasion. Evgeny Vladimirovich was sitting bent over the desk with some book. The thought flashed into my head, "What joy that he is still at least alive and healthy." Something drew me to him impulsively. I came up behind him and kissed him on his bent neck. He turned around. I said: "How I respect you, Zhenya!" I wanted to say, "I love you," but for some reason or other I said respect. It had to be that there was wedged in there the thought that I sympathized with his noble battle in the hospital. He looked at me as if he understood my anxiety for him. He stood up, took me by the hand and, without speaking, we passed through two rooms. Later he said, "I'd like to live with you for twenty-five more years." Under different circumstances I would have been thrilled to hear these words. But now I heard in them the sadness of something that was not to be.

His demands that [the patients'] food be improved did not please the administration, and under the pretext of "unreliability" they sent him away from the hospital and appointed him head of the typhus barracks for Turkish prisoners of war. This was equivalent to a death sentence, since it was well known that older people (older than fifty) do not survive typhus. (In 1915 Evgeny Vladimirovich had reached the age of fifty.) They brought in Turkish prisoners of war and housed them in barracks but gave no money for the battle [against the disease].

Evgeny Vladimirovich, using his own funds, tried to do everything that could be done to battle the infection. Despite his incredible efforts he himself became infected with typhus. We lived then in a dacha on the Ingoda River. I did not allow him to be taken to the hospital, hoping that fresh air and careful nursing would enable him to overcome the illness, although he had turned fifty that year. On the eleventh day the illness was complicated by an edema in his larynx, and Evgeny Vladmirovich died on 2/15 July 1915.[13]

Recently I read Arsenyev's book, *Through the Taiga*.[14] All his descriptions of his journeys make a good impression on me, the more especially because his loving attitude toward both people and nature shines through his sincere words. This time a particular trace of the description of an experience Arsenyev had in the Sikhote-Alin Mountains stayed in my memory. On a moonless night he sat on a mountain overlooking a lake. The stars burned brightly in the sky and were also reflected brightly on the smooth water of the lake. Arsenyev felt as if he had broken away from the earth and ended up in the starry world of the universe. All his earthly cares and troubles seemed to become insignificant.

This reminded me of my experiences after Evgeny Vladimirovich's death. It began with the day of the funeral, when I walked behind the carriage with his coffin. In spite of sleepless nights during his illness I walked unconscious of the ground beneath my feet. It seemed to me that Evgeny Vladimirovich's death raised me to some sort of high stage from which I understood life and death in a new way. I could not express this in words, but I felt myself merge with nature and, through nature, with Evgeny Vladimirovich's soul. Not only earthly nature but also the world of stars became close to me. It seemed to me that now Evgeny Vladimirovich had become closer to me; he was not busy for days at a time in the hospital and was now always with me. I experienced this feeling particularly deeply while I was in quarantine for fifteen days, torn away from my family and my work. If I went into the woods I heard Evgeny Vladimirovich's voice in the birds' songs. At night, when I looked at the stars, in their radiance I felt specially linked with Evgeny Vladimirovich's soul. I was reminded how he and I read in our young years Flamorion's novel *Stella,* where real life ends with a fantastic flight into the celestial world.[15] At that time I had jokingly said to Evgeny: "Maybe we won't die at the same time, let's plan now to meet on the most beautiful star, on Sirius." At the end of the quarantine period I expressed what I went through in verse.[16]

Before his illness I undertook to open, through the parents' circle, a kindergarten for children of the mobilized reservists living under difficult conditions on the edge of town, in the area known as Blacksmith's Row. Now after the death of Evgeny Vladimirovich I felt fully convinced that we would open the kindergarten. It was my wish that people would contribute to the opening of a kindergarten rather than giving wreaths for the grave. This was communicated by someone to the editor of the newspaper, and was published along with the obituaries. And in fact there were no wreaths, and the flow of donations to the kindergarten increased. The kindergarten opened in the fall. Irina Konstantinovna Kakhovskaya, granddaughter of the Decembrist Kakhovsky and a political prisoner recently released from prison, agreed to be the director and teacher. She had been freed on the occasion of the amnesty in honor of the three hundredth anniversary of the House of the Romanovs. Knowing her to be a high-principled, self-sacrificing person, I was sure of the success of this new cause, unusual at that time—the collective education of preschoolers. In preparing materials for occupying the children we used Montessori's book, *The Children's House,* as our guide. Kakhovskaya truly succeeded in setting the work up at the necessary high level. Within a few months the wild, hooliganistic [*dikovatye, khuliganistye*] little children of Blacksmith's Row were unrecognizable; they busied themselves with drawing and modeling enthusiastically, took their [housekeeping] duties seriously, learned children's songs, and so on.[17]

The progressive Chita intelligentsia got the idea of opening two more kindergartens. I was able to organize courses for preschool teachers, which

about forty women students attended. It was essential to rally all those interested in questions of popular education in one society. But it was impossible to obtain permission to open such a society under the tsarist regime.
Before the war we had listed ourselves with an officially existing Petersburg
society (with Kartsov as president) and opened an affiliate of that society
under the modest name, "The Parents' Circle." Members of the circle succeeded in finding money not only for the kindergarten but also for Sunday
schools for adults. Three divisions of the Sunday school were opened in
different parts of town. All the teachers worked without pay. The people
who came to this work were inclined toward revolution. The administration viewed the Sunday schools with suspicion, and there were rumors of
their threatened closure.

At that time Mikhail Vasilevich Frunze arrived in Chita from exile.[18] He
came to me as head with the suggestion that he give a lecture with a revolutionary content for the students [of the Sunday schools]. I described to
him how things were, and he agreed with me that his lecture would provide
a pretext for shutting the Sunday schools. One of the divisions of the Sunday schools moved to the community center [narodnyi dom] that opened at
the same time. The community center did not have its own building; it
rented space in a merchant's house. For some reason or other I do not
remember any details about the opening of the community center. I only
remember that in addition to the Sunday school a drama circle functioned
in it, one of the more active members of which was Ivan Petrovich Kozhikov.
I also remember that in the period of Semenov's regime [Semenovshchina]
Alexandra Davydovna Terekhovskaya and I hid the most valuable equipment of the community center so that the Semenovites would not get it.
Alexandra Davydovna was an active member of the Parents' Circle. She
took the equipment somewhere for safekeeping. After the October Revolution she went to Moscow and became a distinguished worker in preschool
education there.

In the spring of 1916 I. S. Krivonosenko, a physician's assistant, came to
me as a doctor with the proposal that we study Lake Areisk, which according to him was located at the summit of the Yablonov Range; it was renowned among local inhabitants for its curative properties. He and his wife
were born in that region and knew of many cases where seriously ill persons were cured at the lake when previous medical treatments had not made
them better. Krivonosenko had begun to try to get the lake studied a long
time ago and had asked many doctors, but because it was so far away no one
had agreed to go there. Making use of vacation time, I decided to go study
the lake, paying my own way. Others helped me: the physicians' department of the regional administration furnished me with a requisition order
[okrytyi list] for passage on horses belonging to local inhabitants, and the
settlers' administration presented me with a gypsum thermometer for measuring altitude, and a canvas tent. From Krivonosenko I knew that the

lakeshore was uninhabited and that the closest village was seventeen versts from the lake. I. S. Krivonosenko volunteered to accompany me on his own horse. I took my ten-year-old daughter, Lyusya, with me; Krivonosenko also traveled with his twelve-year-old daughter. Thinking over the trip, I set my-self the following goals:

1. make a description of the lake: its size, depth, altitude (with the aid of the gypsum thermometer);
2. observe the characteristics of the water (color, smell, whether gases were given off);
3. evaporate a large quantity of water there in order to bring sediments to the Chita laboratory;
4. arrange for the special dispatch of water to Chita to investigate radio-activity;
5. bring algae, mud, and so on, to Chita; [and]
6. observe the sick: the illnesses they are treating and the course of their illnesses.

We only managed to live at the lake for six days. Downpours started, the tent got drenched, and a messenger was not able to get any food at the near-est village. All this forced us to leave in spite of a generally favorable impres-sion of the lake. I included all the data from my observations in an article on my return. It was published in the local medical-veterinary journal.

A talk on Lake Areisk that I gave to the Chita society of physicians stimu-lated great interest. The conclusions I presented in my talk were as follows: Lake Areisk is an excellent place for a sanatorium; my observations of those who were taking the waters and examination of the cured indicate that the gaseous waters of the lake and the other curative properties contribute to the rapid healing of purulent wounds and speed the closing of bone fistu-lae from tuberculosis. I proposed first opening a sanatorium at the lake for children with bone tuberculosis.[19] The medical inspector undertook to so-licit funds to cover the initial expenditures (the construction of barracks) for the future sanatorium. Soon after this I learned that the funds had been allocated and that on 3 March 1917, I could obtain three thousand rubles. I. S. Krivonosenko had already come to an agreement with the carpenters who were to build the barracks. The parents of children ill with bone tuber-culosis asked me to take their children to Lake Areisk, promising that they would help to equip the barracks and feed the children.

Revolution and Civil War in Chita

The February Revolution drastically changed life, and the issue of the sana-torium died away. . . . [*sic*] Each day brought staggering news; a humble teacher, Khrisanf Matveevich Simakov, leading a detachment of Cossacks, invaded the governor's house and arrested Governor Kiyashko. A Committee of Public Safety was organized, among whose many members my brother Nikolai, a former inmate of the Schlüsselburg prison, and I were elected.[20] The Socialist Revolutionaries played the leading role in the committee. Before each meeting of the committee they went off into a special room and conferred among themselves for a long time, and in so doing earned the displeasure of the other members who had gathered. Meetings and demonstrations started in the town. In the field of public education a regional school council [*sovet*] was created, with V. V. Polivanov elected president. The Transbaikal Teachers' Union elected me vice chairman for adult education. I had twenty-two thousand rubles at my disposal, in addition to which I found out that the former director of elementary schools [*narodnykh uchilishch*] had transferred several thousand rubles to Sytin Press in Moscow for an order of reactionary literature. A directive had to be sent by telegram to stop that order, and a new list of books had to be sent.

In my area twenty places were designated where reading rooms [*izby-chital'ni*] and Sunday schools needed to be opened. In Chita I bought up all the appropriate literature in bookstores and distributed it to the reading rooms. We had to select young teachers of a revolutionary frame of mind to organize and run the reading rooms. All this work so captivated me that I attended neither meetings nor demonstrations, and spent all my time at the school council in a room filled with piles of books.

Members of the SR and SD [Socialist Revolutionary and Social Democratic] parties each tried to draw me into their party but I refused, saying that that would distract me from work that I considered the most important for restructuring life. When one [member] of the Bolshevik Party, in making such a suggestion, pointed out that by entering the party I could work on public education with greater success I was very confused; while I sympathized with the Bolsheviks, at the same time I knew that I was not suited to become a party member. One of my shortcomings was that I always evaluated people according to their moral qualities and not according to their political convictions. I loved Kakhovskaya as a daughter and could not regard her as an enemy although she belonged to the SR Party.[21] Another of my shortcomings was my characteristic tearfulness, with which I tried to battle, unsuccessfully, all my life. In real grief I did not shed tears, on the contrary my eyes felt dry, but in the face of some offense, even a trifling one, tears would fill my eyes and fall like rain in bad weather. I would have disgraced myself with tears at party meetings in the face of any kind of painful criticism. In response to the proposal I rather incoherently said that I was more interested in psychology than politics, that I preferred to work in the rear and not in the front lines. With this I ruined myself in the eyes of party folk, and they gave up on me as a bad job. But there undoubtedly was a need for the kind of worker I was. It was proposed that a high school for adults be opened in Chita with funds from the cooperative,

Fig. 4.2. Anna Nikolaevna Bek with her daughter, Lyudmila (Lyusya), 1913.

with the full program of a gymnasium. I threw myself into this idea, and on 9 December 1917, the school, called "Evening Classes for Adults," opened.

Busy exclusively with community work, I gave little time to my daughter, Lyusya, but I was not worried about her since my brother Innokenty's whole family of six had come to our house from Petrograd. With them came A. I. Serebrennikova with her 9-year-old son. A happy din filled the house, and Lyusya was not alone. Innokenty was interested in organizing the pioneers (at that time they were still called scouts). He was named their elder comrade and imparted a cultured slant to the behavior of his own and others' children. Thus Lyusya came under a good influence.

In 1918 Soviet power came briefly to Chita. The Regional School Council was turned into the Public Education Committee. I continued to head its Department of Adult Education. A former teacher, Mikhail Petrovich Malyshev, presided. In September the Semenovites seized power and the business of adult education ended. Evening courses for adults continued, but there were always rumors that the Semenovites were threatening to destroy the courses as a center of revolution. Everything was plunged into the darkness of reaction. The town was filled with Japanese. Persecutions of

Bolsheviks began. M. P. Malyshev and another eminent Bolshevik, Taube, hid in our house for a time. Semenov himself was a native of the Aksha District, he knew the love and authority Dr. Bek had enjoyed among the Cossacks, and people said he ordered my name crossed out on a list of people to be arrested. At one time the arrests ceased, and Malyshev and Taube came out from our "refuge," but they were soon arrested and sent to prison. Taube was executed, but Malyshev was sent to the prison in Verkhne-Udinsk.

The kindergarten continued to function, but I. K. Kakhovskaya was not there. As soon as the February Revolution had taken place I. K. said that she would not work at the kindergarten. I begged her in vain to wait till we found another director. At my words "How can you not be sorry to desert the poor children?" she answered, "I'm going to fight for the socialist revolution so that there won't be any poor children." After a few days' interruption the kindergarten began to function under a new head, L. N. Elbakyants. She was a member of the Bolshevik Party.

One incident from the first days of the revolution comes clearly to mind, when I found myself at a meeting of prostitutes. One evening a smart carriage drawn by a black trotter drew up to our house. The coachman gave me a note signed "Prostitutes," which earnestly begged me to come to their meeting. This interested me, and I decided to go. Fearing some sort of incident, my brother, Nikolai, offered to accompany me. Arriving there we entered a large room where I was struck by the large number of prostitutes that had gathered. Young girls filled several rows of chairs. Among them a group of Japanese women in national dress with odd hairstyles stood out. It was clear they were waiting for me. A middle-aged woman, not like a prostitute, opened the meeting. She was probably the wife of a brothel keeper [*soderzhatel' pritona*]. She spoke about the new authorities' decree closing all legal houses of prostitution.[22] Throughout her speech she tried to elicit my sympathy for the "poor young girls who live well here, while they want to push them out onto the street, to go hungry and fall into need." Turning to me, she asked me to intercede for them, to petition that the decree not be implemented. After her a beautiful young woman spoke, who said that she had finished six classes of a gymnasium. Her mother had not accustomed her to any kind of work. When her mother died she had no money, she did not know how to work, and she now could live only in this kind of establishment. Taking the floor, I expressed my negative attitude toward their shameful life. I informed them that the government would not chase them out onto the street but rather was opening a dormitory with different kinds of workshops where they would be taught to live by honest labor. Silence fell after my speech, and then the quiet voice of one of the girls could be heard, "I want to leave here to get married." The meeting ended. From the dejected faces I saw that they had not expected this from me; this was expressed also in the president's voice when she announced the meeting closed. They did not give us the trotter to take my brother and me home, and we returned on foot at night along the muddy streets on the outskirts of town. I laughingly said with my brother that it was better to go by foot than to go by the brothel keeper's trotter. Later we learned that during the time of Semenov's regime such houses flourished. The Semenov officers' club was located next to our house in a big stone, two-floor building. Drunken voices and the sound of dishes carried from there into our yard, and drunken officers, cursing as they left the club, cut down young trees planted in front of our house with their sabers.

At the end of 1919, during Semenov's regime, I applied to the Department of Health and was appointed to head the Chita regional hospital for the mentally ill. This forced me to study psychiatric literature in earnest to prepare myself to look after the mentally ill. I had to conduct work with the hospital personnel to eliminate cruel measures in patient care, for example beating [patients] with plaited straps [*zhgutami*], rolling them up in sheets, and so on. The selection of two nurses turned out to be very successful; both were interested in psychiatric literature, and related to the patients with sensitivity. One incident clearly comes to mind. There was one strong man among the patients, a worker named Babkin. Once he fell into a violent state and threatened to kill the attendants. Three attendants succeeded with difficulty in dragging him to the isolator. There he fell into an even more violent frenzy. He succeeded there in tearing a thick beam from the wall and began to strike the door with it with all his might, so that the door began to crack. The terrified attendants, fearing that the door would not hold, called me. One of the nurses, named Vassa Nikanorovna, went with me. This cumbersome name did not coincide with her youthful, pleasant appearance. In discussing what measures to take against Babkin's unruliness, she suggested that she should go in to him without the attendants with a treat and calm him down. I agreed, knowing from earlier experience that Babkin related well to nurses.

A glass of tea, white bread on a plate, and pieces of sugar were brought in. Vassa Nikanorovna's pink face with its childishly cheerful blue eyes, with golden curls surrounding the white hat on her head, the white smock—all this had a touching, calming appearance. Through the door, V. N. said affectionately, "Babkin, I brought you a treat." The blows against the door ceased. I told the attendants to hide after unlocking the door, that only Vassa Nikanorovna and I would enter the isolator. The door opened. It was a terrifying moment: the powerful Babkin stood with the raised beam in his hands. Upon seeing Vassa Nikanorovna with the treat in her hands he was clearly struck dumb and made some kind of clumsy motion, as though he wanted to bow before Vassa's tiny little figure; the weapon in his hand began slowly to fall to his side. I went up to him without speaking, took the heavy beam from his hands without resistance, and took it out into the corridor. On my way out I heard Babkin's coarse voice: "Thank you, little Sister!" It was a vivid lesson for the attendants in how good can conquer evil.

At the beginning of November 1920, when Semenov's regime was liquidated and Soviet power established once and for all, I was called from the
psychiatric clinic to the health department to manage the department for
the protection of mothers and children.[23] The organization of day care,
prenatal and postnatal centers, and so on, interested me less than adult
education, for which the coming of Soviet power opened great possibilities. Shortly thereafter I moved again, from the health department to the
public education department.

A state university opened in Chita. Our evening courses for adults were
turned into a *rabfak*.[24] During Semenov's regime the course continued to
exist thanks only to the voluntary labor of the entire staff. Now Soviet power
began to pay liberally for the pedagogical work of all these teachers. But I
did not have long to work in Chita. Lyusya finished high school. She had to
be given the opportunity to get a higher education. Chita State University
was moved to Vladivostok. I wanted Lyusya to get a medical education, but
she did not want to be a doctor and applied for admission to Irkutsk
University's natural science department.

In addition to my desire to be with her, the possibility of working in psychology attracted me to Irkutsk. I knew that child psychology and defectology,
that is, the study of various deviations in child development, had been introduced into the program of the School of Education [*pedfak*]. By that time I
had collected considerable material, and by working with Chita's teachers I
saw that the investigative approach to schoolchildren was interesting to teachers and useful for them in their practical work. My application for an assis-
tantship in the Department of Psychology was strengthened by my two
published works on the physical and psychological causes of children's failure to succeed in school. I was accepted in 1923. I was sorry to leave the
evening courses (now the *rabfak*), with which so many pleasant memories
and tough experiences during the period of the Semenov regime were associated. I wrote a farewell letter from my whole heart. It was read at a general
meeting of the students. On the day of my departure the students brought
me a testimonial that was also full of good feelings. At the end of the testimonial it said, "Only the hope of meeting you within the walls of higher education soothes somewhat our regret at your departure from our family."

In truth, in later days while working in Irkutsk I used to encounter my
former students from the *rabfak*. Just recently I learned that the former car-
penter Oparin is now a Ph.D. in science [*kandidat nauk*] in the Irkutsk medical school. He worked on phytopathology in the region of the Urov disease,
and now works in pharmacology in an institution of higher education.

Lyusya was accepted into the Irkutsk School of Education [*pedfak*] and
left Chita before me. My *rabfak* students accompanied me to the station
and warmly bid me good-bye.

Verses

In memory of Evgeny Vladimirovich
(On my feelings about his death [1915])

You are indeed alive! You did not leave the world,
Although they buried you in the ground forever.
You are indeed alive—the starry lyre told me so,
The earth whispered this wordlessly.

When in the moonlight rows of clouds
Form a beautiful pattern
You are indeed alive, in them I see without words,
In them your tender gaze shines on me.
We always shared our thoughts,
We lived as two, but had one life.
And life was cut short . . .
Your tomb remained . . .

When with grief over this unequal battle,
I fall on your tomb toward you,
"Don't grieve, he's with you,"
The fragrant stockflower says to me.

Whether I go along the shore, or hurry from my thoughts into the forest,
Everywhere I sense nature anew:
The songs of birds, and forest sounds,
And the majestic river current, as if it were caressing the water.
Everything has become close to me:
Indeed, you went away into nature.
You left life a friend of the people
Through the fault of the tsar's servants
You sacrificed yourself in service to society,
And stood many times for the rights of the people in unequal battle.

You were thrown into the backward, distant Cossack land,
Branded "Dangerous to the tsar's power."
Many exiles, powerless, lost heart in those hard years.
You did not, but mounted the path of research.
Your labor made a valuable contribution to science.

Relating warmly to people, you relieved their suffering,
Returned vision to the blind,
And far from the powers that be, quietly
Dedicated your strength to enlightening the people.

The loss is deeper than my own tears, in grieving for you,
I cannot say: "You're mine."
The people's love for you
Depicts your image more vividly,
In the battle, in the work,
The living memory of you will remain.

5.

The Highs and Lows of Working Life: Irkutsk, Novosibirsk, Tomsk

Anna Nikolaevna devotes the final segment of her memoir almost entirely to her professional career as a research scientist and university professor. Permeated with love for her work and a sense of pride and accomplishment, this chapter describes her ascent to a professorship at the University of Tomsk, the "pinnacle" of her life. Compelled to leave the profession of teaching and her chosen discipline of psychology by Communist Party decrees imposing scientific orthodoxy, she ends her memoir with a brief chronicle of her gradual retirement until she stopped working entirely at age seventy-six, having descended "by stages to the narrow family role of grandmother."[1]

Her experiences as a scientist and professor in Irkutsk, Novosibirsk, and Tomsk provide unique and valuable insights into the history of science in the USSR in the 1920s and 1930s. Her account reveals how individual teachers and scholars at provincial institutions of higher education outside the major centers of Moscow and Leningrad participated in the vigorous scientific debates of the 1920s, and how the battles between different schools affected their views and careers. This chapter also demonstrates the Communist Party's increasing interference in academic disciplines after 1929, and its growing control over what was taught and by whom. Finally, the academic world Anna Nikolaevna entered was dominated by men. Describing her encounters with hostile male students, self-aggrandizing doctors, and jealous male colleagues, she reveals herself to have been an independent thinker, receptive to new trends and ideas in psychology and pedagogy, and unafraid of challenging the "old-boy network" and the scientific and Party establishments.

Dominant trends in psychology in the 1920s and early 1930s in the Soviet Union made the discipline particularly attractive to Anna Nikolaevna. In addition to integrating her expertise and experience in medicine and education, psychology allowed her to pursue her strong interest in Marxist philosophy, empirical research, and social activism. Though still a relatively young discipline, psychology was thriving in the Soviet Union in the 1920s.[2] In the comparatively free cultural climate of that decade, different schools engaged in unfettered and lively debate over the nature of human consciousness and the influence of biology and the social environment on human thought and behavior. Even before the 1917 Revolution psychologists had argued over whether psychologists should take a philosophical, "subjective" approach to studying the mind or look for the origins of behavior and thought in "objective" physiological processes or environmental conditions. Enthusiasm for the work of such early psychophysiologists as Ivan Sechenov, William James, and

Hermann Helmholtz, and especially for the work on reflexes by physiologists Ivan Pavlov and Vladimir Bekhterev, lent support to a strong biological trend in theories about the psyche in Russia, a trend that intensified in the early Soviet period. In the 1920s diverse theories competed for general acceptance as Soviet psychologists sought an authentically Marxist understanding of the mind that would also serve the communist goal of an entirely new kind of human society.

Anna Nikolaevna participated actively in these debates. She embraced the discipline of "reflexology," which almost replaced the study of the mind per se in Soviet psychology during the 1920s. Reflexologists asserted the primacy of biological and physiological factors and processes in explaining human behavior. Supported by the discoveries of two of Russia's most eminent scientists, Pavlov (who had won the Nobel Prize) and Bekhterev, reflexology seemed also to accord with Marxism's materialist, objectivist, and determinist approach. As the lecture she gave in Chita in 1914 demonstrates (see the appendix), Anna Nikolaevna had become interested in psychophysiology and reflexology even before the revolution. So it is not surprising that, arriving in Irkutsk in 1923, she immediately introduced the new discipline into her course on psychology. Her victory in the debate over reflexology with senior colleagues in 1924 and her appointment as head of the psychology department in 1927 reflect the ascendancy of physiological and behaviorist approaches in Russian psychology in the 1920s. By the end of the decade, however, reflexology had come under attack. In January 1930, at the First All-Union Congress on Human Behavior, psychologists objected to reducing the psyche to physiology and neglecting human consciousness as an independent and purposive influence on human behavior.

Another new discipline, pedology, experienced a similar heyday in the 1920s and early 1930s, and exerted a powerful influence on both psychology and education in the Soviet Union. Drawing from medicine, psychology, and sociology, pedologists sought to integrate studies of physical, mental, and social development in order to gain a holistic understanding of the child. They employed an experimental approach that sought quantitative data derived from tests and experiments to explain child development and behavior. Like reflexology, pedology stressed the primacy of external influences—biological, social, environmental—on mental processes and development. And like reflexology, pedology initially seemed to accord well with Marxism's stress on the influence of material conditions on behavior and culture, and with the Soviet goal of educating young people for socialism. As chapter 5 reveals, Anna Nikolaevna's academic research and teaching came to focus on this new discipline.

An article written by Anna Nikolaevna in 1928, entitled "On the Transitional Age," illustrates pedology's interdisciplinary approach to questions of child development and the methodologies pedologists employed.[3] Writing for teachers and parents, she analyzes the physical and psychological changes of puberty. She uses students' journals, compositions, interviews, and even her own experience as a parent to examine adolescents' concepts of themselves, their changing goals, and their relations with their parents and other authorities. She studies students' ideas about friendship and love, and their experience with members of their own sex and later with members of the opposite sex. Her underlying subject throughout is the interrelationship of physical, mental, and behavioral changes during puberty.

Receiving official endorsement from the Commissariat of Enlightenment in 1931, pedology reached the peak of its influence over pedagogy and psychology in the early 1930s, when Anna Nikolaevna arrived at Tomsk University to head its psychology and pedology department. Shortly thereafter, however, the status of pedology as a discipline began to decline. The leading journal *Pedologiia* stopped publication in 1932. A 1934 decree cutting the number of hours allotted to pedology in the curriculum signaled that the discipline had come under official disapproval. Finally, on 4 July 1936 the Central Committee of the Communist Party issued a decree, "On Pedological Perversions in the System of the People's Commissariat of Enlightenment." This decree labeled pedology a "pseudo-science" and condemned it for the extreme environmental determinism of its explanations of child behavior and for its failure to produce practical means for improving education. The party required pedologists to denounce their discipline publicly.

The attacks against reflexology and pedology and their decline as academic disciplines demonstrate the increasing interference of the Communist Party in science and higher education from 1930. Party control over what constituted scientific orthodoxy became increasingly stringent and openly applied. As Anna Nikolaevna's own experience demonstrates, local party officials also gained power to control personnel by forcing their retirement or causing their public humiliation.

Anna Nikolaevna's memoirs say very little about the much broader conflicts and upheavals that shook the country outside the university during the 1920s and 1930s, even though their repercussions can be seen in her experiences as a professor and scholar. By the end of the 1920s the Stalin faction had solidified its power in Moscow, and under its leadership the Communist Party approved the policies of rapid industrialization and complete collectivization. Forced grain requisitioning had been introduced in Siberia in 1928, giving rise to armed opposition and even a number of serious peasant revolts. These were hushed up and suppressed with the use of the army. Forced industrialization resulted in the rapid construction of new enterprises and the expansion of industrial production, but speed and lack of planning resulted in enormous waste, environmental damage, and a drastic decline in workers' standard of living. At the same time the press, controlled as all media were, sang the praises of new industrial enterprises and collective farms. As the 1930s progressed the Communist Party imposed ever more stringent controls and stepped up its persecutions of class enemies, "wreckers" and "saboteurs," and former or imagined political opponents.

Although Anna Nikolaevna was not a party member, she could hardly have been unaware of the immense changes the Soviet Union experienced during Stalin's "revolution from above." What did she know in those years of the First

Five-Year Plan, 1928–1932? Did she not hear of the appalling conditions on the industrial construction sites? Did she not see or hear about the hapless peasants fleeing collectivization, ducking the label of "kulak," arrest, or exile? Some city persons could conceivably claim they knew nothing if they kept their eyes narrowly on their professions or family life, but Anna Nikolaevna traveled into the country to do research, and it is highly unlikely that she saw or heard nothing about the consequences of forced grain requisitions and rapid collectivization. Like most Soviet citizens she was also directly touched by the purges and terror of the 1930s. Compelled herself to leave Irkutsk and later to resign because of her "incorrect" political views, she also had friends and relatives who were arrested, including her brother, Nikolai, who died in a Stalinist labor camp.

Whatever she read, saw, or heard did not find its way into her memoirs, and it is difficult to discern the impact of these national events on her life and her views. Writing in 1948 at the height of Stalinism, perhaps she was afraid to write anything that could be construed as critical of the Communist Party, even in a private memoir, since such criticism might endanger her family if it became known. Perhaps as a Marxist who shared the Russian intelligentsia's faith in economic and social progress, she supported the party's economic policies and goals while regretting the human costs. The experience of World War II may also help to explain these omissions, since the Soviet victory seemed to vindicate the party's decisions and the centrally planned and managed economy that they created. Although Anna Nikolaevna scarcely mentions the war, it was still fresh in her memory at the time she began writing her memoirs. Novosibirsk, where she lived during the war, was far from the front, but the war still greatly affected the region. Streams of people migrated from European Russia to Novosibirsk, a major evacuation and relocation center, and whole factories were disassembled and shipped there by railroad to be rebuilt and put into wartime production. As the war dragged on shortages worsened in all areas, and food rations shrank; workers such as Lyusya and her husband received 800 grams of bread a day, while elderly people like Anna Nikolaevna and children received only 350 grams. This meant that the Andrusevich household of three adults and four boys received about 3 kilograms of bread daily. They supplemented this with vegetables they grew and stored in the cellar, and a cow and a pig for milk and meat. Living conditions continued to be very harsh after the war ended in 1945.

The end of World War II corresponded with the end of Anna Nikolaevna's working life. Influenced by her upbringing, her own natural ambition, and the emphasis that the Russian intelligentsia and Soviet ideology placed on labor and service to society, Anna Nikolaevna had strived to work and contribute productively to her society throughout her life. It was difficult for her to accept the physical limitations of old age and leave the workplace for private life.

MEMOIRS

Recollections of Life in Irkutsk, 1923–1930

At Irkutsk University I initially experienced hostility from the students.[4] The staff was being purged of ideologically unsuitable teachers at that time, and because of the purge the head of the Department of Psychology, Professor Rubinshtein, had just been fired.[5] He was renowned as an outstanding lecturer and enjoyed great authority among the students, especially among one group of women students who were called ironically the "myrrh-bearing women."[6] Professor Rubinshtein based his psychology course on idealistic philosophy. He took the students away from the concrete, material world in his lectures and failed to give them guidance appropriate to pedagogical practice, whereas Marxism requires that you go from concrete phenomena to abstraction and from there to practice. Lenin called for the study of everyday phenomena with particular insistence so that in analysis one would come to know their laws of development and know how to change what was undesirable. He spoke about the necessity of "beginning from what was simplest, widespread, encountered a million times in life," and discovering dialectical laws.

After Rubinshtein left I was assigned the upper-class course on defectology (deviations from the norm), directly connected with psychology.[7] I, a woman of modest appearance, arriving from the district, was to replace a famous Moscow professor. This led to the students' hostility toward me. Some of the students, especially the male, reactionary ones, were obstructive: they gave me trick questions, found fault with particular words, and kept me from carrying on with the lecture. Coming from my work with the Chita teachers and having thought deeply about Marxist and psychological literature, I felt the ground firm beneath my feet. After having given a number of introductory lectures and having acquainted the students with the methodology of objective observation (according to Basov), I proposed that each student take one child under observation from the Bekhterev Home, where children who deviated from the norm were housed. Checking and organizing the material they collected, I built a theoretical course on it. Children with various kinds of developmental defects often figured in the lectures.

Students gradually became interested in the experimental method as the course proceeded. Several brought children who deviated from the norm from private homes to study. One woman student said to me, "With Professor Rubinshtein you often sat during the lecture as if you were listening while really your thoughts flew far, far away, and nothing from the lecture remained in your head. At your lectures you do not become distracted."

The next year I was assigned the first-year course of lectures introducing child pedology, that is, the anatomy, physiology, and psychology of the child. I was particularly interested in this course because it gave me the opportunity for a holistic approach to the child without the divisions that used to be common: doctors studied the body and psychologists the psyche, with no interest in bodily development. To me as a physician interested in psychology, the task of combining all the accumulated physiological and psychological knowledge was appealing. The works of Ushinsky and literature on psychophysiology (James) made this possible.[8] The brilliant discoveries of the Academician Pavlov in the field of conditioned [conditional] reflexes provided a bridge between physiology and psychology. I studied the works of Pavlov and Bekhterev with enthusiasm and introduced reflexology into my course. The students responded to my lectures with interest, but the Marxism department and the dean of the *pedfak* [School of Education] sounded the alarm. At that time Academician Pavlov was in conflict with Soviet power, he was debarred from teaching, and his teachings were not recognized. I was warned, but I was deeply convinced of the tremendous significance of reflexology to the materialistic worldview and continued to inform students of the facts of reflexology.

The psychology department challenged me to a debate. The day and hour of the debate were widely posted throughout the university. The student body was interested, and probably the audience would have been enormous, but for some reason the designated time for the debate was changed, and then, without much notice, assigned to a small auditorium in the Medical Institute. When I came to the debate, the auditorium was overflowing, people were even standing in the corridor in front of the doors. The presidium was made up exclusively of opponents of reflexology. I was worried, although I had prepared myself a great deal for the debate. I had collected many excerpts from Marx, Engels, and Lenin, guessing in advance what the possible charges would be. During the debate I answered every accusation with citations from the classics. For example, there was this accusation: "You, contrary to Marxism, reduce psychological phenomena to the physiological." I quoted Lenin in answer: "For every materialist, sensation is the direct connection of consciousness with the external world, it is the conversion of energy from the external stimulus to the fact of consciousness." And another quotation: "Sensation depends on the brain, nerves, retinas, and so on, that is on matter organized in a fixed way" (Lenin, *Materialism and Empiriocriticism*).[9] In response to the accusation of biologism: "Marxism recognizes the psyche as an exclusively social phenomenon, but you speak about the development of the brain equally with the influence of the environment." I quoted Marx in his letter to Kugelman, where he talks about the mutability of thought depending to a degree "both on the maturity of development and in part on the maturity of the thinking organ," that is the brain.

That is the way the whole debate went. From it I became convinced that Marxists know the classics only in relation to their views on the development of society, but they do not know what the classics say about human development. At the conclusion of the debate the chairman of the pre-

Fig. 5.1. Gathering of pedologists at Irkutsk University, 1925 or 1926;
Anna Bek is seated, second from the left.

sidium, Professor Odintsov, expressed the view that reflexology is a young science but that the future belongs to it. I took this as my victory. In my lectures I included information on reflexology as before. Later, I became convinced that my superiors' distrust of the direction of my work had not fully disappeared. Nevertheless, in 1925 I received notification from Moscow that I was promoted to senior lecturer in psychology. In 1927 I was appointed head of the psychology department and was sent for scientific research to Moscow and Leningrad.

I came into contact with the medical world in Irkutsk in 1924 thanks to an Eastern Siberian doctors' congress that took place there. The congress organizers proposed that I, as Dr. E. V. Bek's collaborator, give a talk on the Urov disease. They explained that the first talk on this disease would be given by Professor Shchipachev and that my talk would supplement it. I answered that, before agreeing, I would talk with Professor Shchipachev. Shchipachev answered my questions by saying that his talk needed no supplement of any kind, that he would talk about Dr. Bek's work exhaustively and would even quote him. I was relieved and told the organizers not to include my talk on the agenda. Attending Professor Shchipachev's talk on the designated day, I was flabbergasted [at what I heard]. He reported on the symptoms of the disease very superficially, spoke of his trip to the center of the disease as if he were the first to begin the study of this disease, and, in the whole talk, he did not mention the name of Dr. Bek once, although he clearly used information from his work. In addition to everything else, he said that he had become interested in this work as a result of an assignment given by Professor Kaufman in Berlin. After his talk I took the floor and expressed my amazement and indignation. In conclusion I said, "In Berlin Professor Kaufman knows of Dr. Bek's work because E. V. Bek's dissertation was partially translated into German and the photographs were published in a journal on radiology, yet Professor Shchipachev did not find it necessary even to mention Dr. Bek." A complete scandal ensued. The congress resolved to hold an extra session on Sunday and hear my lecture. I prepared it carefully. Lyusya and Dima Zhukov helped me create the tables. My lecture went well before a full audience.

Taking advantage of the increased interest in the Urov disease, after the congress I raised the question of organizing a special commission with the medical department to study this disease. A commission was soon formed under the chairmanship of the same Professor Shchipachev, and I was chosen secretary. The commission organized expeditions every summer to the endemic center. I went in 1925 as a member of the expedition to the village of Turov, and in 1926 to the village of Korovino. I published the results of my research in an article in a Moscow journal.[10] In the village of Korovino I conducted child anthropometry and began experiments with white mice. In one cage I gave mice plain water and in another boiled, even partly purified, water. With this experiment I wanted to clarify the character of the harmful agent in the water. If the mice on unboiled water exhibited any kind of pathological changes, that would mean that something living was causing harm. If, on the other hand, this happened among the mice on boiled, partly purified water, that would mean the harmful agent had a chemical character. For personal reasons I could spend only one month in the village of Korovino. Just at the end of my stay in Korovino two researchers arrived from the Moscow Institute of Microbiology. I made the mistake of giving them my experiment to continue. They promised to continue the experiment and send me the results of pathological-anatomical investigations from Moscow. In response to my repeated inquiries they refused, saying the research was unfinished. When I was in Moscow on a business trip and spoke personally with them, I gathered from their contradictory answers that they had not continued the experiment. I prepared the results of the child anthropometrical study for presentation at a congress of endocrinologists in Moscow, but Professor Shchipachev presided there. He did not allot time for my presentation. Probably he was influenced by the fact that I had more than once spoken out against his superficial research and unfounded conclusions. Shchipachev was considered a good surgeon in Irkutsk. Another professor in Irkutsk (Shevyakov) said about him: "Shchipachev has golden hands but he is a blockhead."

So my research on children was not published anywhere. In response to his request I sent Dr. Damperov, director of the Urov Scientific Research

Institute, all the archival materials from Evgeny Vladimirovich's work and his unpublished materials, but it is clear from information that I recently received from Dr. Sergievsky that either Damperov never received the package or that it was lost somewhere.

While I was in Irkutsk the following articles of mine were published in the collected works of Irkutsk University:

1. "The Process of the Development of Thought" in 1925;
2. "How to Monitor the Development of the Child in the First Three Years of Life" in 1930;
3. "Contemporary Trends in the Study of Human Behavior" in the jubilee collection of Irkutsk University in 1928;
4. An Irkutsk University commission on relations with teachers published a booklet, *Basic Landmarks in Sex Education,* in 1929;
5. The journal *Siberian Education,* no. 7/8 (1928), published my article, "On the Transitional Age."

I taught pedology in various courses for teachers and instructors in Irkutsk and Novosibirsk where I was invited to give lectures. Having a large network of ties to teachers not only in Eastern but in Western Siberia, I was creating an interest in research on schoolchildren. To satisfy the demand among teachers I myself printed out blank forms for [recording] the characteristics of the schoolchild, and reprinted Binet's scale for studying the degree of children's mental development.[11] I distributed these materials for cash on delivery to various places in response to requests and thus offset the cost of printing. At the *pedfak* I managed to use the funds allotted for laboratory equipment both for [the laboratory's] external appearance and for obtaining all the devices necessary for studying movement dexterity (based on the Ozeretsky scale for studying motor skills [*motoriki*]), and various instruments for psychological experiments. In 1929 the new university rector, Georgy Trifonovich Chuich, who knew me from the *pedfak,* paid particular attention to my laboratory and gave it a flattering review.

In spite of all this the clouds were again thickening over my head. Once again the question came up, was I not deviating from Marxism by linking reflexology with psychology? My assistant, Alyakrinskaya, who had been chief of the "myrrh-bearing women" under Rubinshtein, expressed great interest in my lectures. She was in her last year when I began to teach in the *pedfak.* At that time there was a purge of students. As the daughter of a priest she was threatened with expulsion, but with her good looks she succeeded in captivating a Communist who was on the purge committee. She married him, openly saying to her friends that she was marrying without love. As a successful graduate of the *pedfak* and the wife of a Communist she got a job as assistant in the pedology department when she graduated. Failing to investigate her past carefully, I trusted her fully and believed in her sincere enthusiasm for my direction in child development. But shrewder people later told me about her careerism and hypocrisy. She had an interest in my departure, wanting to take my place herself. Wearing the face of a well-wisher she told me in secret that the new chief of the city's education department was raising the question of dismissing me because, contrary to Marxism, I was working biologism into my lectures.

This was unlikely, since the chief of the city's education department did not have direct ties to the university and, not attending the *pedfak*, could not himself, as a new man, judge the direction my lectures were taking. But at that time it did not occur to me not to believe Alyakrinskaya's words. My family circumstances led me to thinking about leaving Irkutsk. In 1926 Lyusya had gotten married and in 1930 already had two children.[12] Her husband was named a research fellow of the Animal Husbandry Institute in Novosibirsk. Lyusya had left with the children to join him, and I remained alone in Irkutsk. With respect to housekeeping I was completely taken care of by Sofia Ivanovna Cheremisinova, who, starting in Chita, had lived with me continually, but my attachment to Lyusya and my grandsons compelled me to hurry to them.[13] Alyakrinskaya's suggestion about a threat of dismissal provided the final shove, and I offered my resignation for family reasons. I left Irkutsk during vacation time. I do not know how the students would have felt about my departure, but I believe that, among the students, too, some would be found who were pleased with my departure. I knew that in the Komsomol cell there were those who were unhappy about my strict attitude concerning exams.[14] In those days it was accepted for students to take exams as a group.[15] If there were some knowledgeable individuals in the group, then even those who said nothing also received a good grade. I demanded knowledge from each member of the group. That was not popular. Someone speaking about my strictness characterized it with these words: "On the way to her exam, even members of the Komsomol cross themselves."

On the whole I left Irkutsk with a light heart, completely unlike my departure from Chita. Our relative Antonina Ivanovna Serebrennikova was sincerely distressed by my departure.[16] When I left Chita she followed after me and moved to Irkutsk with her son. She took me to the station with a bouquet of flowers and tears in her eyes. Alyakrinskaya also considered it her duty to escort me. Instead of words of regret in farewell, she said, "You are leaving at the right time."

Still, my seven years of work in Irkutsk did not pass without a trace. After I left, Professor M. F. Belyaev, by education purely a psychologist, headed the Department of Pedology and Psychology; I heard from Irkutsk students that after my departure he also began to introduce reflexology into his course and even make reference to my work. Alyakrinskaya gave the pedology course after I left, but the students were dissatisfied with her teaching and she had to leave.

Half a Year in Novosibirsk

As soon as I arrived in Novosibirsk I was invited to be in charge of the pedology laboratory at two institutions, the Institute of Communist Education [*Komvospitanie*] and the Institute for the Protection of the Health of Children and Adolescents.[17] The first was located in the House of Lenin, the second nearby in the Central Polyclinic. Again I faced the task of uniting research on the physical condition of children with the level of their social development, that is, with their psychic development. Both laboratories needed to be equipped. When the work in the laboratory was well in hand, the Institute of Communist Education sent one hundred adolescents—juvenile criminals from some labor colony—for physical evaluation. All of them had been expelled from school at some age. Being interested in the influence of abnormal vision on failure in school, I asked the eye doctor to look not just for near-sightedness as was usually done but also for congenital far-sightedness. In Whipple's manual I had at one time read in the notes, in small print, that congenital far-sightedness has a negative effect on schoolwork. I myself had one near-sighted eye and the other congenitally far-sighted. I always read with the near-sighted eye. When I shut the near-sighted eye and used the far-sighted one, I could not read long. It did not hurt, but I experienced a sort of restless feeling that made me stop reading. In Chita, while studying schoolchildren who were failing, I often found that some had congenital far-sightedness. An interesting result came of this: 67 percent of the juvenile criminals had congenital far-sightedness. The second most common ailment I encountered was adenoid growths in the nasopharynx. With adenoids breathing was difficult, and the children had to breathe with their mouths half open. This made it difficult for them to pay attention for very long, since close attention is accompanied by slowed breathing, so that gave them further difficulty. These abnormalities, discovered in time and eliminated in one case by wearing glasses and in the other by an operation, could positively affect the fate of schoolchildren.

We were also sent children from private homes for study. Children with symptoms of hysteria often turned out to be difficult to bring up. It was interesting to identify all the mistakes in upbringing that led the children to hysteria or other nervous diseases. The tasks before the laboratory were complex and difficult ones, but interesting. Meanwhile G. T. Chuich, who briefly had been director of Irkutsk State University, was sent to Tomsk to organize a pedagogical institute there. Learning that I had left the Irkutsk pedagogical institute, he sent me, by special ambassador, an invitation to come to Tomsk to head the Department of Pedology and Psychology there. I had no desire to drop the work I had just started, especially since Lyusya and her family lived in Novosibirsk. But G. T. Chuich was energetic and persistent. He began to work through party organs. One day the director of the Institute of Communist Education called me into his office and informed

me officially that I was being sent to Tomsk to conduct a course on pedology there. I took that as a personal insult. "That means that they do not
value my work, that I'm not needed here." But I did not say anything out
loud since I sensed that I was not mastering my innate reflex to an insult—
my eyes were filled with tears. I hurriedly left the office. The next day party
member N. Ya. Kostesha, a teacher from Tomsk, upon meeting me said,
not without irony: "What an honor for you! Yesterday at the meeting two
cities argued over you. Tomsk pulled you to itself, but Novosibirsk would
not yield. But Tomsk won anyway." These words showed me that I wrong-
fully had taken offense about something that was necessary to the work.

In February 1931 I arrived in Tomsk. Sofia Ivanovna remained in Novosibirsk with Lyusya. She did not like to move about; she always had a hard
time getting used to a new city and new living conditions. "When you get
settled there, then I'll come," she said. She was an extraordinarily conscien-
tious and honest person. Her personal life was unsuccessful, and she was
sincerely attached to me.

Recollections of Life in Tomsk, 1931–1934

I worked in Tomsk for four years.[18] The first three years went so well for me
that this period could be called the pinnacle of my ascent up the stages of
public life. I was beautifully situated materially, especially when the pedagogical institute moved from Semashko to Kiev Street into a large two-story
stone building. I was given a big room on a side corridor. In the same corridor I had a room for my pedology and psychology laboratory, and a third
door led into my lecture hall. It turned out to be a comfortable private
residence for me. The students and administration treated me in a friendly
way. At the end of my first year I was selected for professorial rank. At that
time professors were selected in all institutions of higher learning by their
own professorial collectives. I began to be called "Professor Bek." I was not
vain but being selected was nice for me, of course. One of my first thoughts
was, "How pleased my father would be if he were alive." My psychology
course, including information on reflexology, no longer met opposition
since Pavlov's teachings had been recognized and his discoveries were [now]
acclaimed as works of genius. With the coming of the third, decisive year of
the Five-Year Plan I was awarded a certificate of merit from the party professional organizations and the administration of Tomsk University as "an active and conscious fighter for the Bolshevik tempo of work and study, and a
shock worker in socialist construction." It seemed that everything was going well, but it did not turn out that way. . . . [*sic*]

At the beginning of 1934 a new head of the *diamat* [dialectical material-
ism] department appeared, Comrade Laizan. On the face of it he was a
pleasant, good-natured person, not like an introspective philosopher. He
considered it his job to organize a circle on dialectical materialism among

the scientific researchers. I signed up for this circle immediately and attended all its meetings conscientiously.

I had had a penchant for philosophical studies since my youth. I was worried about the question of the meaning of life. My older sister, Tanya, at sixty-seven years of age, wrote in a letter to me shortly before her death, "Is it possible that I will die without understanding the meaning of life?" I too wanted to know. Without getting into mysticism, I wanted to comprehend all that exists, especially the question of the psyche, that is, the human soul. It seemed to me that our earth is a little grain [*krupinka*] in some infinitely great Universe. The point of life on earth is in the development of living things from the simplest to a human being. The point of the life of a human being must be the development of the psyche. The human brain as complexly organized matter reflects the earthly world, accumulates knowledge, thinks; and human thought creates something new in the various spheres of social life (creativity in art, science, technology, and so on). Life is a battle for life. Man uses his creative energies in the battle for his personal life, for the life of his descendants, for the life of humanity. Is it possible that this wonderful psychic energy manifests itself only on our modest planet, Earth? Is not the soul of every person an atom of the creative energy disseminated throughout the universe? There, thought breaks off.

Entering the *diamat* philosophy circle, I expected new material to help me make sense of life. After several meetings of the circle I spoke my mind to Comrade Laizan; what the circle was doing was boring and unproductive. Comrades' talks consisted of long, bare readings of dialectics (selections from a reader) without substantive content. If these same laws of dialectics, together with their formulation, were disclosed on the basis of materials from various disciplines, then there could be a lively exchange of opinions in the circle. I expressed these thoughts after Comrade Laizan's talk on the subject "The Theory of Knowledge." My statement was received in cold silence. Discussions of the talk were conducted exclusively on the question, "Is the psyche material?"

To my astonishment representatives of the *diamat* department affirmed that the psyche is nonmaterial. This was idealism. I gave them quotations from the works of the Marxist classics, where it is clearly stated that there is nothing nonmaterial in the world, and, what is more, by the word "matter" they mean not crudely physical matter, but everything objectively real and accessible to study. They [Marxist classics] brought up the example of radio waves; they are not matter in the physical sense yet they exist objectively and are accessible for study. Or another example, a person's reflection in the mirror is not matter in the crude sense but it is an objectively real phenomenon studied in physics. But my opponents stuck with their point of view. Half-jokingly I said: "If you convince me that the psyche is not material, then coming into the circle a materialist, I will go out a Hegelian." At the end of the discussion three persons were singled out to put together resolutions. The next day I left for Moscow at the invitation of a congress of endocrinologists. Returning from Moscow I was astonished to learn that in my absence there had been a general meeting with mandatory attendance by all students and the professor-teaching staff. It was specially called to unmask my errors. At the meeting they read the resolutions on the discussions at the meeting [of the circle]. These resolutions were printed in the Pedagogical Institute's newspaper; in them they ascribed to me every deviation from Marxism that existed in the philosophical world. It was curious to read that at one and the same time they ascribed contradictory positions to me, such as mechanism and subjective idealism, vulgar materialism and Kantian agnosticism, they even ascribed the theory of symbols and hieroglyphs to me.[19]

Even stranger was that in these resolutions the authors pointed out my serious work on questions of Marxism-Leninism in the field of pedology. At the same large gathering, in my absence, they criticized my printed works, taking individual phrases out of them and interpreting them arbitrarily. Lina Zhukova was at this meeting and took detailed notes. From her notes it is clear that from my little book, *How to Monitor the Development of the Child in the First Three Years of Life,* they took the sentence where I say that "in day care centers for the infants of workers an environment has been created that is as positive for the child's development as that which formerly was available only to the bourgeoisie." From this they drew the conclusion that I was calling back the bourgeois order. Only Comrade Laizan and the secretary of the party cell, Comrade Akimov, spoke against me. The chairman of the general meeting asked the students to point out the deviations from Marxism in my lectures on pedology. But only two of the students raised their hands in answer. One asked, "Why is Bek being criticized in her absence?" The other said that they had noticed no deviations in the lectures of A. N. Bek.

No conclusions were made about my teaching activity at the general meeting. Learning all this, I did not even feel offended, the accusations were too baseless and senseless. It seemed to me that the *diamat* department disgraced itself more than me. Meeting Comrade Laizan in the corridor one day I calmly said to him, "If you had ever been to my lectures on pedology you would not have imputed such contradictory deviations to me." He did not answer, but I saw embarrassment on his face. Nevertheless, I had to react somehow to what had gone on. G. T. Chuich, no longer director by then but only head of the language department, advised me to write to Moscow to the party Central Committee, to Comrade Stetskoi, who, according to Chuich, was specially assigned to review conflicts in institutions of higher education. I took this advice and detailed all that had happened in a letter. Having sent the letter, I calmed down and carried on with business as usual.

But a heavier blow was waiting for me. In the new [academic] programs received from Moscow half as many hours were allotted to pedology as before, and practical work in pedology was completely removed. In this I saw the decline of pedology as a science. I was reminded of two congresses on pedology in earlier years. At both congresses there had been heated discussions between psychologists and pedologists. The psychologists, with Professor Kornilov at their head, denied the significance of pedology and said that individual specialists in anatomy, physiology, and psychology should study the child.[20] The pedologists insisted on a holistic approach to the child. They pointed to geography as a science; like pedology, it studies a complicated subject using information from different sciences. They pointed out the shortcomings of psychology, which studies the psyche in general, tearing it away from the bodily changes related to a person's age. The discussions became a passionate, hostile polemic. One got the impression that this was not a battle for life but to the death. And here there appeared threatening signs in the form of drastic reductions in hours for pedology. Clearly pedology would remain an insignificant appendage to pedagogy.

I wanted to leave Tomsk University altogether and return to Novosibirsk. Practical people advised me not to leave without obtaining my academic pension. I already had the right to one. One needed ten years of work in an institution of higher education and twenty-five years in public education. I had eleven years of work in an institution of higher education and more than thirty years in public education. In applying for the right to an academic pension it was necessary to present a reference from the party organization about one's most recent work. I approached Comrade Akimov, and he gave me the kind of reference that made it impossible to request a pension. There was much flattering talk in the reference about my teaching and social activity, but at the end it said, "but she did not fight for the party's general line." I had to give up any thought of a pension. But after a while I was suddenly asked to return this reference and was given a new one instead, entirely complimentary. This evidently happened thanks to my letter to Comrade Stetskoi. I was later told that the party organization received something from Moscow that forced it to give me another reference. So I sent in my application with all the necessary documents and, as a result, in March 1934 I received an academic pension of 250 rubles. At the end of the school year I went on holiday and submitted my resignation.[21]

Life in Novosibirsk Again

Giving up work in Tomsk, I spent the summer with Lyusya's family at the Barlaksky state farm thirty kilometers from Novosibirsk. Toward autumn it was necessary to arrange for work. My previous job in Novosibirsk did not exist: the Institute for the Protection of the Health of Children and Adolescents was closed; the Institute of Communist Education still existed but there was no pedology laboratory. I was offered work in the regional health department as head of the methodology laboratory in the Department for the Protection of Children's Health. I set to work here and became interested in the task of publishing an anthology of articles on questions of work in sanitary [*ozdorovitel'nye*] establishments. A collective was organized of doctors and pedologists, who distributed the topics for articles among themselves. I headed up this collective. The chief editor was party member Tolstunova. I did a preliminary editing of the articles and did all the work with the press. I was very pleased when, in the spring of 1935, our anthology emerged from the press in great stacks, and it was possible to distribute them to workers going out to sanitary establishments. There was great demand for the anthology.

But here, too, grief [*ogorchenie*] befell me. The anthology was forbidden because the introduction that Tolstunova contributed, it turned out, was not in line with political circumstances. People came to us expecting the anthology but left with empty hands. There was yet another grief. The regional health office organized a congress on questions of protecting children's health, at which representatives from Moscow and from various Siberian cities assembled. I was supposed to give a talk at the congress on the work of children's polyclinics. I had begun to investigate the work of polyclinics on my own initiative and had worked up a large quantity of material for the talk. I had had to rework my talk a number of times on the instructions of the chief editor Comrade Tolstunova. At the end of the revisions there was very little of mine left in it. The congress sessions began at eight in the morning and, after a break, continued to 10:00 in the evening. My talk, for some reason or other, was set at the very end, that is, about 10:00 in the evening.

I did not go home during the break because I lived far away. Toward evening I felt great fatigue. I was not decisive enough to refuse to give the talk, and when I went out on the stage I sensed that all the corrections that Tolstunova had made had flown out of my head. I could not read my manuscript, because the lighting in the large hall in the regional executive committee's building was too diffuse for my weak eyes. I had difficulty making out even the charts that were supposed to illustrate my talk. My situation was tragic. I began to speak about the results of my research, not only without any of the [earlier] corrections, but I also introduced into the talk what I wanted to tell school doctors from my own experience, that is, information that had not been in the talk that had passed through the chief editor's censorship. Finishing my speech, I felt completely stupefied. Tolstunova criticized something, protested against something, and someone else criticized data in my talk. It was all the same to me. Recalling the failure of the anthology and now, as it seemed to me, the flop of my talk, I decided to draft my letter of resignation from work the very next day.

Before this, I had been asked to teach psychology at an evening pedagogical institute. I had agreed willingly. I had thought I would finish my life teaching. In addition to the evening pedagogical institute I was asked to give a psychology course in the program for school inspectors. It seemed that

Fig. 5.2. Ceremony in Aksha in honor of the Beks, mid-1990s. The plaque that was placed on the Beks' house there reads, "From 1906 to 1912 the well-known physicians and social activists of the Transbaikal Evgeny Vladimirovich and Anna Nikolaevna Bek lived in this house."

I would again land on the path I had blazed of lectures on the development of the human psyche, beginning with childhood and devoting special attention to the psyche of schoolchildren. But here, too, fate turned things against me. The announcement that pedology was a politically harmful science and the persecution of pedologists—almost like that against the enemies of the Soviet order—fell like thunder from a clear sky. Although I was teaching psychology, as a former child development specialist I would be required to disavow pedology in print and point out the harmfulness of the science. I could not do that in good conscience, and, for refusing, I was fired from teaching psychology. The path of teaching was closed to me forever.

But every cloud has a silver lining. It was time for me to remember that I was a doctor, that I had spent so many years acquiring medical knowledge and until now had worked so little at my basic specialty. I went to a children's clinic and was taken on there as a pediatrician. I had to sit down again with the literature to refresh my knowledge of children's diseases. In addition to seeing patients my responsibilities included in-depth examinations of schoolchildren in various schools of the October District. I had ties to schools once again. Still, in reviewing my life, I consider this period a step down.

I worked in the October children's polyclinic seven years altogether. The last year, during the second fatherland war, I was working as doctor in the industrial trade school belonging to the "Trud" factory. I worked there one year.

Walking the long distance from our house to the "Trud" factory was difficult for me. My daughter's family lived on a stock farm where she insisted I move.[22] I became a medical worker in the day care center there. I liked working in the day care center. I was interested in the subject of "the development of social indicators [*proiavleniia*] in children of day care age." The day care center collective, after a number of conversations, made up its mind to observe and identify the [indicators of] sociability of children (joint play and occupations, aid to each other, and so on). The nannies and director reported their observations to me, and I made notes of everything.

After a year the position of medical worker was terminated because of staff reductions. I had to leave. It was the last stage in my working life.

Appendix

"Labor Education and the Montessori System" Summary of a Lecture

Anna Nikolaevna Bek

[The following is a] brief summary of a lecture I presented in 1914, re-created from memory. The lecture evoked great public interest at that time and served as the stimulus for the organization of a pedagogical society and the establishment of the first kindergarten in Chita. My memory has retained only the basic ideas that I have reproduced here. My exposition of them at that time was undoubtedly livelier. While living in Aksha I studied psychological and pedagogical literature a great deal. While so doing, and reading the classics, I picked out everything that had a close relationship to real-life practice. In psychological literature I studied James's "psychophysiology" and Longe's "The Results of Science" with particular interest.[1] In pedagogy I read Ushinsky and his student, Vodovozova, and Lesgaft.[2] Traveling to Petersburg I stocked up on contemporary literature there. Many thoughts had accumulated in my mind in connection with my own observations, and I wanted to share them with parents and teachers. I did not read this lecture from notes but spoke, pouring out all that I had been thinking over. I had only a general outline of what I wanted to say in my mind. The words poured out from deep in my soul and probably that contributed to my influence on the public.

Issues of childrearing [*vospitanie detei*] should interest not only parents and teachers but also every member of the community. The well-being of life depends a great deal on the mental [*dushevnykh*] qualities of individual members of society. An extraordinarily important question is whether children in a given society will develop into loafers, hooligans, and future criminals or, conversely, will be brought up to be intellectually developed, industrious, and benevolent people who relate honestly to their obligations. In order to educate properly, pedagogues themselves have to be on a high level of development, they must understand what natural laws should lie at the foundation of education. In other professions, for example, in the technical professions, knowledge of the laws of physics, chemistry, and other [sciences] underlies the organization of the work process. Educators must know the laws of the development of mental qualities. The science of the psyche [*nauka o dushe*]—psychology—until recently could not discover a single law that could be used in practice. In spite of its venerable age, psychology was sterile because the human psyche was considered God's heavenly gift; it was thought that it did not depend on the body or the environment. Psychologists thought that the psyche could be studied only in and of itself, that is, subjectively. The closer you come to our time, the more scientists there are who understood the dependence of the psyche on the body and who studied change in mental states in relation to changes in the state of the body. They have strived to create the new science of psychophysiology (James, Wundt) and their research has produced something valuable. But our Russian scientist Sechenov gave an even more fruitful stimulus to the science of the psyche; he made the brilliant discovery that the psyche develops under the influence of the environment as a reflection in the brain of everything that a person sees, hears, and experiences. He formulated this with the words "the psyche is reflexes of the cerebrum [*golovnogo mozga*]." The word "reflex" in translation means reflection. This discovery of Sechenov was met at the time with distrust and was soon forgotten. Laws of the higher nervous activity of the brain were discovered anew in our time by the famous physiologist Pavlov. At present, his students and followers are working out the new science of reflexology. Experiments in which laws on the reflection of external influences in the brain are being discovered are so convincing that they leave no room for distrust.[3]

Without going deeply into this teaching let us take as a demonstration two types of children from classical literature.[4] On the one hand, in Nekrasov's "The Little Peasant Lad" [*Maliutka muzhichek*] we have little Vlas, virtuously bringing wood from the forest for his family. At his age (eight years old) he should be running and playing, but he understands his duty; clearly he feels for his mother and little sisters sitting in the cold hut and hurries to bring them firewood.

Let us take, on the other hand, Goncharov's type, Ilyusha Oblomov.[5] He is a noble landowner's child. In the gentry milieu, sated idleness was considered to be happiness. Work was a disgrace for them, a punishment from God for the sins of Adam and Eve. A "noble" person, according to them, should use the labor of others; servants, as people of a lower order, should work for him; the treatment of servants had to be haughty.

If we compare the mental qualities of Vlas to those of Ilyusha we find in the early years that they share many traits characteristic of childhood. Both want to run, play, do something. But the older they get and the longer they are subject to the influence of their environment, the more they will differ in their mental qualities. These two types bespeak the decisive influence of the environment on the human development.

The hereditary gifts of both young boys could be the same; but there exists a natural law that that which is exercised will develop in the child [and] that which is not exercised will weaken and die away. All data from observation and study of the psyche indicate that the mind is not given to the human being in a finished state, that all mental qualities develop under the influence of surrounding life. It is impossible to reeducate a child unless all earlier influences on him are changed. Educational measures must correspond to the child's age characteristics. The life of a human being from birth to maturity develops according to natural laws, going from one stage to another: nursery, preschool, younger and older schoolchild. During this time appearance changes, needs and interests change, the child's entire conduct changes depending on the stage of development of the organism, and in particular on the stage of brain maturation. The brain of a newborn differs sharply from the brain of an adult owing to its unfinished structure. The gradual maturation of the brain expands the child's capacity to become acquainted with life around him and to acquire habits.

In preschool years three traits most characteristic of childhood behavior manifest themselves with particular clarity, that is, play, imitation, and curiosity. Healthy children of any nationality, any social class, in any country try to play under any circumstances. In play they imitate the people they see. In imitating, children do not make judgments about what is good and what is bad. Hearing choice swearwords, children repeat these swearwords as willingly as any other. In the countryside on holidays I have had the occasion to see how children imitated drunks: they stood in a line, embracing one another, and went down the street swaying back and forth like drunks and sang in drunken voices. The curiosity of children is well known generally. They stick their noses everywhere.

Curiosity, games, and imitation, as the law of the child's nature, lead to the fact that children, observing life around them and reflecting it in their games and imitations, learn to live in accordance with the customs and traditions of a given society. In outdoor games, with their various rules, children develop strength and dexterity. At the same time, observing rules of the game develops their ability to govern themselves, to limit themselves. Work made a person a person. The absence of work in the life of Ilyusha Oblomov deformed his personality. His environment taught him to value only sated idleness and made him lazy. Children's games of imitation should be looked at as the preparatory stage to labor activity. The character of children's games changes according to their age. The writer Korolenko, in his book, *The History of My Contemporary*, gives these characteristics of early school-age children: "cheerful, free from care, running about in the fresh air, noisy comradeship, and balls flying through the air."[6]

Games in the nursery and preschool periods have a different character. The most primitive game of a baby is, on seeing a metal spoon, grabbing it, licking it, and then banging it on the table. This banging clearly satisfies the baby, he can repeat it a hundred times. Such intensive play develops hand muscles and acquaints the child with the sound of metal, with its hardness, and so on. Preschoolers' games can be very diverse. Children are particularly pleased with movement games with singing, which develop the whole organism. At home preschoolers' high activity often annoys adults whom the children hinder in their daily tasks. Adults are inclined to consider the sedentary child "intelligent." True, the normal activity of children has some limits. Excessive activity, when the child cannot keep still for a minute, indicates nervousness, an abnormal condition of his nervous system. And inactivity makes one think of illness (rickets, anemia, and so on).

The most extreme degree of inactivity is observed in idiots, in whom brain maturation stops soon after birth because of an inherited burden (syphilis, parents' alcoholism).[7] Such children do not know how to play or imitate, and do not exhibit curiosity. Their activity is limited to reaching for food and knowing how to grab something so as not to fall. The French physician Séguin (in the middle of the last century) made up his mind to develop idiot children, to make them, at least at some level, acceptable in society.[8] In the course of many years of persistent labor, and after trying various approaches, he came to the conclusion that "the development of muscles leads to the development of the mind." The idiots had to have their muscles developed under compulsion. Thus, for example, Séguin's experiment with stairs. If a normal preschool child sees a staircase he will start to climb it without fail. Séguin forced the idiot child to go up and down the steps. In order to do this he put a wide belt on the child with a ring at his back. Raised by the ring the idiot hung in the air and instinctively grabbed for the staircase. Persistent, daily exercise led the idiot in the end to know how to climb up and down. In the same way, over the years, the idiot learned other expedient movements. As a result of motor development, some signs of the mind (understanding) appeared. To develop the mind, Séguin created different game materials and made the children use them. Thus the idiots learned to discern size, form, the color of objects, and so on. The development of motion under compulsion at first evoked wild cries from the idiots. Séguin's enemies denounced him, charging him with torturing the children. After Séguin had worked many years a committee was sent to check on him, on the basis of the denunciations. Members of the commission saw a group of children doing gymnastics. To their question, "Where are the idiots?" Séguin could answer with pride: "These children were idiots."

A student of Séguin's, the Italian Maria Montessori, having adopted Séguin's ideas, decided to apply Séguin's play materials to normal children, with some modifications.[9] The normal activity of preschoolers in conditions of group education can take the form of unruly pushing of one another, fights, and so on. For the development of expedient movements a series of devices was introduced: short staircases, jump ropes, swings, games with balls, movement games with musical accompaniment. In order to develop work habits, self-service by the children was strictly enforced and they took turns on duty in the cafeteria. Here, in the illustrations I have set up, you see a series of play materials designed for the development of mental activity: making estimates by eye, observation skills, familiarity with geometric figures, and so on. Among the play materials there are large letters cut out of sandpaper. By tracing these letters with their fingers, four-year-old children learn to write them and then to read.

As early as the middle of the last century Froebel advanced the idea of the group education of preschoolers.[10] He gave the name "kindergarten" to such institutions. According to Froebel, the task of preparing children for labor activity was also basic to preschool education. Therefore Froebel allocates great attention to developing children's creative abilities, abilities that develop by drawing, sculpting, cutting from paper, building with blocks, and movement games accompanied by music.

According to the opinion of many thinker-pedagogues, foreign as well as Russian, the preparation of children for work through play should continue in school as well, where, along with play and physical exercise, real labor should be introduced gradually in the form of different trades. In Russia Ushinsky and Lesgaft were especially prominent champions of the ideas of labor education in school.

In conclusion, let us return to our two types of children—to Vlas and Ilyusha. Let us compare them at a mature age. In his work Goncharov showed clearly how much Oblomov's personality was deformed by his lordly education. In spite of adequate intellectual development he was helpless, unable to overcome the least little obstacle. Even such a strong emotion as his love for Olga could not rouse him to activity. Oblomov's lot was to drag out a pitiful, colorless existence, unworthy both of him personally and of society.

With respect to Vlas, it is easy for us to imagine two possibilities for his development. If he continued to live in a poor peasant family, without access to education, his personality would not receive full development, but through his work he would bring benefit to his family and society. The plausible tale of the famous satirist Saltykov-Shchedrin, "How the Peasant Fed Two Generals on an Uninhabited Island," speaks to us about the peasant's significance.[11] Not only did the peasant feed them, he delivered them home from the uninhabited island.

Another possibility for Vlas: if after childhood he wanted and had the opportunity to get an education, he could achieve much as he was accustomed to working. Lomonosov serves as an example.[12] Growing up in a working family, tempered by his battle with the harsh natural world of the far north, he began to study at nineteen years of age and not only mastered existing scientific knowledge but also furthered science himself.

We live in an age that has seen the emergence of true objective science about the laws of the development of the human personality. Despite the fact that this science has taken only its first steps, it already promises future successes.

We parents, teachers, and educators have the obligation to observe and study children and to try to discover conditions and methods for their higher development.

Notes

Notes by Adele M. Lindenmeyr are marked "A.M.L." All other notes are by Anne D. Rassweiler.

INTRODUCTION

1. George Kennan (1845–1924) was the uncle of diplomat and historian George F. Kennan (b. 1904).

2. Anna Nikolaevna Zhukova-Bek's memoirs were first published together with the medical dissertation written by her husband, Dr. Evgeny Vladimirovich Bek, on a bone disease endemic to the Transbaikal region; Evgeny Konstantinovich Andrusevich, ed., *Obshchee Delo* (Novosibirsk: Sibirskii khronograf, 1996). Anne Rassweiler's translation includes sections from the manuscript of Anna Nikolaevna's memoirs that were not included in the 1996 edition published in Russia.—A.M.L.

3. Valentin Rasputin, *Siberia, Siberia,* trans. Margaret Winchell and Gerald Mikkelson (Evanston, Ill.: Northwestern University Press, 1996); originally published as *Sibir', Sibir'* (Moscow: Molodaia Gvardiia, 1991).

4. The Decembrists were young aristocrats and military officers who staged an unsuccessful revolt in 1825 to force the monarchy to introduce a constitution and abolish serfdom. Dostoevsky spent almost ten years in Siberian prison and exile for his participation in clandestine radical circles in St. Petersburg in 1848–49. Polish revolutionaries were exiled to Siberia following the unsuccessful revolutions in Russian Poland against imperial rule in 1831 and 1863; they included the parents of novelist Joseph Conrad. In 1771–73 Cossack Emelyan Pugachev led a mass uprising of Cossacks, peasants, religious dissenters, and others against Catherine the Great and serfdom in the region along the Volga River.

5. See chapter 5.

6. See chapters 1 and 5.

7. See chapter 4.

8. In the archives and museums that Anne Rassweiler visited in Chita she examined official records pertaining to the medical careers of Anna Nikolaevna and her husband, the public health reports he wrote about the Cossacks and convicts living in the territory where he served as district physician, and the history of the town when the Beks lived there.—A.M.L.

9. See chapter 3.

10. See chapters 1 and 3.

1. Growing Up in the Transbaikal

1. It was probably her father's position, for example, that enabled Anna Nikolaevna to attend the elite school in Irkutsk that restricted admittance to daughters of nobility or high civil servants, since both her parents had come from quite humble origins.—A.M.L.

2. George Kennan, *Siberia and the Exile System*, 2 vols. (New York: Century, 1891), 2:323–24.

3. We can only wonder what happened to that diary. It was not among her possessions.

4. In 1771–73, along the Volga River, serfs and Cossacks led by Emelyan Pugachev revolted against the monarchy, taxes, serfdom, and religious persecution. The Russian army finally quashed the rebellion by 1773, and Pugachev, brought to Moscow in a cage, was executed; participants in the revolt were also either executed or sent to hard labor in Siberia.—A.M.L.

5. Grushenka is a nickname derived from Agrafena.

6. Established in 1870, *Niva* was a family-oriented, apolitical, and illustrated weekly magazine, aimed at a mass readership from Russia's emerging middle classes across the huge empire, such as the Zhukovs. Its popular scientific articles, household advice, and especially its fiction—*Niva* published the works of scores of Russian and foreign writers, and their collected works appeared in the free supplements—won it immense popularity in late imperial Russia.—A.M.L.

7. According to Russian folk belief, mischievous spirits inhabited the house, barn, bathhouse, and other parts of a peasant farmstead.

8. *Izbushka* is a little *izba*, or peasant log house.

9. This section was not in the original chapter 1 of the memoirs but was written by Anna Nikolaevna later.

10. 1 *sazhen* = 2.13 meters.

11. As indicated in the introduction to this chapter, *Ivan Bezrodnyi* and *Ivan Nepomniashchii* were names common among Russian vagrants.—A.M.L.

12. *Omul'* is the name of several varieties of fish in the salmon family found in Siberian rivers and Lake Baikal.

13. Anna Nikolaevna's memoirs resume at this point.

14. Appointed by the tsarist government, school inspectors had broad powers and also responsibilities over the primary and secondary schools in their district.—A.M.L.

15. Ivan S. Turgenev's controversial and influential 1862 novel, *Fathers and Sons*, explored the generational conflicts, student radicalism, and progressive ideas of the liberal decade that followed the accession of Alexander II to the throne in 1855.—A.M.L.

16. On the Higher Women's Courses, which provided university-level education to women, see chapter 2.

17. This section from Anna Nikolaevna's girlhood diary is inserted here into the text of the memoirs.

18. July 13.

19. The dropping of the patronymic implies a degree of familiarity that embarrassed Anna Nikolaevna.

20. A verst (*versta*) is the old Russian measure for distance, equal to approximately ⅝ mile or 1.06 kilometers.

21. Anna Nikolaevna mentions that the girls and women danced alone at first. This was the custom of the *devichnik*, the dancing of girls and women on the eve of the church ceremony. Later on in the evening, in this case, the men joined in, and the general dancing included set pieces such as quadrilles and individual dances such as waltzes.

22. Anna Nikolaevna's expression of pleasure with her outfit and her looks as a teenager contrasts with her indifference toward dress later in life, when, as a student, a revolutionary, and finally a doctor and teacher, she adopted the intelligentsia's ascetic attitude toward such frivolities.

23. In the Russian Orthodox wedding ceremony the bride and groom stand under special crowns or wreaths.

24. Nikolai A. Nekrasov (1821–1878) was a poet who enjoyed great popularity in progressive circles, especially among students, for his poems devoted to social wrongs and the sufferings of common people, such as "Knight for an Hour."—A.M.L.

25. A progressive journalist and writer, Alexander K. Sheller (1838–1900) wrote poetry, novels, political and sociological essays on education, and other social and political questions under the pseudonym Mikhailov.—A.M.L.

26. Anna Nikolaevna's memoirs resume here.

27. On the origins of women's medical education in Russia, see chapter 2.

28. The revolutionary Peter F. Yakubovich (1860–1911), who wrote under the pseudonym Melshin, belonged to the People's Will Party that had carried out the assassination of Alexander II in 1881. Arrested in 1884, he spent three years in prison and eight years (1887–95) in exile in Siberia. His book of stories about convict life, *A World of Outcasts*, published in 1896, had a great impact on Russian public opinion. Thanks to Anna Nikolaevna's memoir, we learn that the manuscript of this important book was smuggled out of Siberia in the luggage of a twenty-four-year-old aspiring medical student!—A.M.L.

29. Construction on the Trans-Siberian Railroad had begun only in 1892 but proceeded quickly. As this account makes clear, in 1894 travelers from eastern Siberia to European Russia could travel west by train only from the western Siberian city of Tyumen.

2. STUDENT LIFE IN ST. PETERSBURG AND FRANCE

1. By contrast Irkutsk, the largest city in which Anna Nikolaevna had lived before arriving in St. Petersburg, had slightly more than 50,000 inhabitants in 1897.—A.M.L.

2. Organized in large immigrant cities like St. Petersburg and Moscow, *zemliachestva* provided migrants from other parts of the empire with social networks, mutual financial assistance, and contact with home.

3. The question of Anna Nikolaevna's own political views and affiliations is first raised in chapter 2 of her memoir. Several factors may have influenced her early Marxist affiliation, though she does not elaborate on her views here. Marxism, with its claims of having discovered the laws of history, may very well have had greater appeal to her scientific mind and aspirations as a student than the more idealist and utopian strain of radical populist socialism. At the same time, Anna Nikolaevna wrote her recollections during the repressive last years of Stalinism in the Soviet Union, and so it seems unlikely that she would confess to heterodox views or ties in

her memoir. In addition, though never a member of the Communist Party, she had spent a long and productive career as a member of the Soviet medical and educational establishment, although repression in the 1930s cut her academic career short. The complex issue of her politics will arise again in chapter 5.—A.M.L.

4. Olga Palem, a young Jewish woman from a prosperous Odessa family, lived in St. Petersburg with her lover, Alexander Dovnar, whom she supported financially and regarded as her fiancé. In a violent argument at the Hotel Europa in May 1894, she shot Dovnar with a revolver and then tried to commit suicide. Palem's trial on the charge of premeditated murder opened in February 1895 and became national, front-page news for its duration. As Anna Nikolaevna's account reflects, Russian public opinion hotly debated not only the nature and extent of Palem's guilt but also broader issues of women's rationality, men's exploitation of women, mental illness as a defense, and, after the jury declared Palem not guilty, the merits of trial by jury. Palem was tried again the following year and found guilty of second-degree murder, but she received a light sentence. I am grateful to Tatsuya Mitsuda and Alexandra Oberländer for this information.—A.M.L.

5. In 1885–86 the Russian government linked the ruble to the French franc at a ratio of one ruble to four francs. Russia moved to the gold standard in 1897, at which time the ruble was worth approximately fifty cents ($1.00 = 1.94 rubles).—A.M.L.

6. Anna Nikolaevna could not have visited the actual castle of the Bastille, since it was torn down in the late summer and early fall of 1789. She probably visited an attraction popular with tourists in Paris in the 1890s, a panorama of the Bastille during the early days of the French Revolution located on the Place Diderot.—A.M.L.

7. The Franco-Russian Alliance developed in stages during the early 1890s, from a diplomatic agreement in 1891 to a military treaty in 1894; at the same time economic ties between Russia and France increased.—A.M.L.

8. *Pelmeni* are Siberian meat dumplings, similar to ravioli, and *kvas* is a beverage made from bread. *Michel Strogoff* is a novel by Jules Verne.

9. Anna Nikolaevna is alluding to one of the main points of contention between populist and Marxist socialists in Russia. Marxists rejected the populists' faith that the collective traditions and poverty of the Russian peasantry made them a force with powerful revolutionary potential, awaiting only a spark to rise up against landlords and the tsarist regime.—A.M.L.

10. The town of Oranienbaum (now Lomonosov), the location of one of the imperial summer palaces, is on the southern shore of the Gulf of Finland, about forty kilometers south of St. Petersburg.

11. "*A on u tebia kudy sdaden?*"

12. Threatening avalanches are often set off by timed explosions in designated areas to protect the public from their potential danger.

13. "Dubinushka" is a Russian folk song sung by barge haulers and other stevedores as they worked.—A.M.L.

14. A German Social Democrat and member of the Reichstag, Eduard Bernstein (1850–1932) created a storm in the European Socialist movement with his book, *Evolutionary Marxism* (1899), which pointed out that, contrary to Marx's predictions, the standard of living of European workers had improved with the advance of capitalism, and that the right to vote now gave workers the opportunity to work peacefully by democratic means to bring about reform. Bernstein was the most well-known spokesman for the revisionist position in European Marxism, which advocated reform rather than revolution as the means to achieve socialism.—A.M.L.

15. Anna Nikolaevna probably attended the lectures of Alexander I. Vvedensky (1856–1925) of St. Petersburg University, a leader of the philosophical school (as opposed to the experimental, physiological school) in Russian psychology. In chapter 5 she elaborates on her attraction to the objective, behaviorist approach to understanding the human psyche over the subjective and philosophical approach.—A.M.L.

16. In the 1890s the economists Peter B. Struve (1870–1944) and Mikhail I. Tugan-Baranovsky (1865–1919) were prominent members of the "Legal Marxist" wing of Russian revisionist socialism, which applied Marxist economic theories to Russian development while rejecting Marx's predictions of revolution. Struve later became a leading liberal politician. Historian Pavel N. Milyukov (1859–1943) was not a Marxist but a liberal constitutionalist, later the leader of Russia's largest non-socialist liberal party, the Constitutional Democrats, and briefly foreign minister in the Provisional Government in 1917.—A.M.L.

17. Here Anna Nikolaevna refers to A. M. (or Maksim) Gorky (pseudonym for A. M. Peshkov, 1868–1936), the radical author whose stories about Russia's underclass and three-part autobiography had already won him renown by the 1890s.

18. Set in a cheap boarding house for vagrants, criminals, and paupers, Gorky's play *The Lower Depths* sympathetically explored the impact of poverty and injustice on human morality and behavior. Published and first produced in 1902, *The Lower Depths* appeared too late to have been the play discussed by the student circle Anna Nikolaevna describes here.—A.M.L.

19. In 1901 students at St. Vladimir University in Kiev held a large meeting to protest the incarceration of two fellow students; authorities punished 183 of the participants by forcibly conscripting them into the army (students at institutions of higher education were exempt from military service).—A.M.L.

20. On the Trans-Siberian Railroad, see chap. 1 n. 29.

21. This section is not part of the original memoir but was written by Anna Nikolaevna later and appended to this chapter. By "Natasha," Anna Nikolaevna is probably referring here to Natasha Rostova in Tolstoy's *War and Peace.*—A.M.L.

22. The Marxist Russian Social Democratic Labor Party's greatest rival, the peasant-oriented Socialist Revolutionary Party, was founded in 1901 to carry on the populist and terrorist traditions of Russian radicalism of the 1870s. It became the most popular political party in Russia, although its record of terrorist assassinations and lack of organization hampered its political influence.—A.M.L.

3. New Beginnings

Chapter 3, covering the years 1901 to 1912, is a composite of pieces Anna Nikolaevna wrote at different times toward the end of her life. The two sections from the original memoir manuscript included here, "A Year in Nerchinsk Zavod" and "Recollections of Life in Aksha," contain little about her marriage and her relationship with her husband, Dr. Bek. Fortunately she wrote several short recollections that are more personal in tone and content than the formal memoir, and that return repeatedly to the theme of her great love for her husband. Relevant portions of these pieces—"The Life of Evgeny Vladimirovich Bek," "1952," and "On the Adaptation of Men and Women to Life Together as They Enter Marriage"—are therefore incorporated into this chapter.—A.M.L.

1. W. Bruce Lincoln, *The Conquest of a Continent: Siberia and the Russians* (New York: Random House, 1994), 261.

2. In the early twentieth century there were eleven Cossack "Hosts" or forces across the Russian Empire, one of which was the Transbaikal Host. Primarily Russian in ethnicity, Cossacks constituted a distinct social and legal class, with their own institutions of self-governance; for example, Cossack chieftains, or *atamans*, were elected. They formed cavalry regiments of the Russian army and, like the Transbaikal Host, were settled in frontier regions to defend Russian borders; their settlements were known as stations. Both Cossack soldiers and their families fell under military jurisdiction, which is why Dr. Bek, an army doctor, was assigned to serve this population. Buryats are a Mongolian people living south of Lake Baikal on the Russian border with Mongolia. Still largely nomadic under the empire, they practiced Buddhism or shamanism.—A.M.L.

3. "People's houses," or *narodnye doma*, began to appear in Russian towns only in the 1890s, established by social reformers or progressive municipalities to serve the educational and cultural needs of the urban lower classes, or by temperance activists to provide workers an alternative to spending their leisure time in the tavern. A national survey in 1913 found 222 functioning *narodnye doma* in towns and rural districts across the empire (*Narodnyi dom* [Petrograd, 1918], 377).—A.M.L.

4. Posyet is on the Sea of Japan in the Russian Far East, located south of Vladivostok almost on the border with Manchuria.—A.M.L.

5. Nikolai I. Pirogov (1810–1881) was a renowned physician, teacher, and humanitarian reformer who greatly influenced the progressive character of the Russian medical profession; the Society of Russian Physicians in Memory of N. I. Pirogov, founded shortly after his death, was the leading professional association for Russian physicians before the Soviet era.—A.M.L.

6. *Osteoarthritis deformans endemica*, also known as Kashin's or Bek's Disease, was endemic to a large region of the Transbaikal. Usually affecting people in their early teens, the disease causes distinctive deformities of the hands, shortened and deformed legs and arms, joint pain, and premature aging. The causes are presumed to be the region's water or diet (*Sibirskaia sovetskaia entsiklopediia*, vol. 1 [Novosibirsk, 1929]).—A.M.L.

7. She was actually thirty-one.

8. Seven *versts* equal approximately 4.6 miles.

9. *Baryshnia* is a term of address used by peasants and servants for young ladies of the gentry.

10. "The people's darkness" was an expression common among the Russian educated elite. It refers to the common people's illiteracy, their lack of hygiene, their backward culture, and apparent lack of interest in improving their condition.

11. Dobchinsky is one of the comic characters in the satirical play *The Inspector General* by Nikolai V. Gogol (1809–1852).—A.M.L.

12. In his proposal to Anna Nikolaevna Dr. Bek used an affectionate diminutive of her name, and the informal pronoun *ty*, used among family and close friends, instead of the formal *vy* that he and she had been using with each other, as was appropriate for colleagues.

13. For Russians there was no civil marriage or other alternative to marriage in the Orthodox Church.

14. For Gorky, see chap. 2 n. 17; Vladimir G. Korolenko (1853–1921) was a radical novelist and poet who also published exposés of abuses and injustices in the Russian political and legal systems.

15. Dr. Kashin was Dr. Bek's predecessor in his next post, Aksha.

16. The Argun River flows along the Russian-Chinese border into the Amur River.—A.M.L.

17. In other words, out of the Cossack class, whose welfare was the obligation of the Russian army, into the peasantry, for whose well-being the government bore no responsibility.—A.M.L.

18. This was a distance of less than five miles.

19. V. Veresaev, *Na voine: zapiski* (St. Petersburg: Slovo, 1908). Like the Beks, Vikenty V. Veresaev (pseudonym for Smidovich) worked at the front as a military physician. The English translation is V. Veresaev, *In the War: Memoirs of V. Veresaev,* trans. Leo Wiener (New York: Mitchell Kennerley, 1917).

20. Spelled *Vafengchou* elsewhere in the memoir. Anna Nikolaevna is probably referring to the Manchurian town of Wa-fang-tien, on the Liaotung Peninsula, where in June 1904 the Japanese defeated an attempt by the Russian army to relieve the besieged Port Arthur on the tip of the peninsula from the north.—A.M.L.

21. Kung-chuling is a town on the South Manchurian Railroad to Mukden (today, Shen-yang), the old capital of Manchuria, where Russian and Japanese forces fought for almost a month in February–March 1905 before the city fell to the Japanese.—A.M.L.

22. *Russkii vrach*, the leading professional journal for physicians.—A.M.L.

23. The incident is missing in 1908 editions of Veresaev's book, but it is described in the 1917 English translation cited in note 18 above; see pages 182–83.

24. They traveled approximately 233 kilometers, or 140 miles, on horseback.

25. Perun was the pre-Christian Slavic god of thunder, the worship of whom gradually shifted to St. Elijah (Iliya) but who was still present in Russian folk belief.—A.M.L.

26. The land captain, or *zemskii nachal'nik*, was a local government official, usually a noble landowner, a post created in 1889 for the supervision of the peasant population and established in Siberia in 1898 as the *krest'ianskii nachal'nik*.—A.M.L.

27. As a military doctor employed by the Russian state to treat the Cossack military reserves and their families, Dr. Bek received a state salary.—A.M.L.

28. Alexander N. Ostrovsky (1823–1886) was the most popular playwright in Russia in the second half of the nineteenth century; plays such as *Poverty Is Not a Vice* (1854), about the ruin of a merchant drunkard, Lyubim Tortsov, were staged countless times by both professional and amateur theater companies.—A.M.L.

29. One *pud* equals approximately 36 pounds; in other words, it was rumored that the Beks had almost 1,450 pounds of books.

30. Ivan P. Pavlov (1849–1936), winner of the Nobel Prize in 1904, was a physiologist renowned for his experiments with conditioned reflexes; Vladimir M. Bekhterev (1857–1927) was a psychiatrist and neurophysiologist who studied mental disorders, brain function, and conditioned or, in his term, associated reflexes. For the influence of Pavlov and Bekhterev on Russian and Soviet psychology, see chapter 5.

31. Konstantin D. Ushinsky (1824–1870) was Imperial Russia's most influential educational theorist and advocate of progressive pedagogical methods. His major

work, *Chelovek kak predmet vospitaniia: opyt pedagogicheskoi antropologii* (Man as the object of education: An attempt at a pedagogical anthropology), was first published in 1868–69, shortly before his death, and subsequently went through many editions.—A.M.L.

32. In fact, the investigation was not directed at the Beks but at the young woman whose schooling Evgeny Vladimirovich had financed, and who was serving as nanny for their daughter. The police suspected that she was a member of the Socialist Revolutionary Party.

33. The *Domostroi* was a sixteenth-century household manual and guide to everyday religious observance and family life, known for its emphasis on the absolute authority of fathers and husbands over their wives, children, and servants.

34. Anna Nikolaevna probably meant Sretensk, a town on the Amur River accessible by steamship to Khabarovsk, the final station on the Trans-Siberian Railroad.—A.M.L.

35. Hereditary honorable citizen was a legal class established in 1832 for distinguished government officials, merchants, and others of non-noble social status. In fact, the governor awarded honorary citizenship to Evgeny Vladimirovich Bek, but not to both Beks. Anna Nikolaevna apparently never learned of this. The award lies in the state archives in Chita.

4. MAKING A CAREER

1. V. Nemerov, *Chita* (Chita: Chitinskoe oblastnoe knizhnoe izdatel'stvo, 1994), 101.

2. Arrested for revolutionary activity in St. Petersburg, Nikolai Zhukov spent several years in tsarist prisons. He was arrested again by the Soviet government in the 1930s, and he died in a Siberian labor camp. A sculptor and teacher, Innokenty Zhukov moved to Moscow after the civil war, where he also became one of the early activists of the Soviet Scouting movement that became the Young Pioneers (from the Zhukov-Bek family archive and from the recollections of Anna Nikolaevna's daughter, in Boris Tuchin, "Suprugi Bek: Kontseptsiia 'Obshchego dela,'" *Obshchee delo*, 26–28).—A.M.L.

3. Elections to the Constituent Assembly, a national assembly charged with creating a new governmental structure for Russia after the fall of the monarchy, were held across the country in November, but the body met only once in early January before being disbanded by the Soviets.—A.M.L.

4. Born in a Cossack settlement in Transbaikal in 1890 of a Cossack father and Buryat mother, Semenov served in the Russian army through World War I on the western, northern, and Caucasian fronts. When the Bolsheviks seized control of Transbaikal he raised a multiethnic force in Manchuria, receiving assistance from Britain, France, and Japan. This Special Manchurian Detachment seized Chita in October 1918, and Semenov declared himself the ataman of the "Provisional Government of Transbaikal." He stayed in power in Chita for two years, supported militarily by the Japanese. In exile he eventually settled in Dairen, where the invading Soviet Red Army arrested him in August 1945; he was tried for anticommunist activity in Moscow in 1946 and executed.—A.M.L.

5. Memoirs by Anna Nikolaevna's daughter and brother, the city archives, and local newspapers make it possible to fill in some of the details of her life in Chita during the years of war and revolution.

6. The titles of the articles were "Physical Causes of School Failure" and "On the Psychological Factors Influencing Children's Success in School."

7. Édouard Séguin (1812–1880), a French-American physician and psychologist, became a pioneer in the education of the mentally retarded. Like Anna Nikolaevna, Maria Montessori (1870–1952) was a physician (the first woman to receive a medical degree from the University of Rome) who turned to education, psychology, and child development. The system she developed that bears her name stresses creating school environments where children are encouraged to exhibit individual initiative, creativity and self-education, and collective responsibility for general housekeeping chores. "Idiots" (*idioty*) was the standard term used at this time for people with mental retardation.—A.M.L.

8. See chap. 3 n. 30.

9. Anna Nikolaevna's summary of this lecture is in the appendix.—A.M.L.

10. The following three paragraphs are taken from her later writing on marriage, entitled "1952."—A.M.L.

11. It was typical of the tsarist government in the early twentieth century not to allow the independent pedagogical society desired by the lecture attendees. The tsarist government was frightened of civic initiatives and all groups that would allow citizens to come together and possibly discuss antigovernment activities. By opening a branch of an association that already had a legal charter, those wishing to set up the society bypassed the need for an officially approved charter. Thus they became part of a national network of persons interested in improving education.

12. The remainder of this paragraph and the next one are inserted from "1952."— A.M.L.

13. The two dates represent the Julian and Georgian calendars; with the revolution, Russia moved to the Georgian calendar. An edema is a swelling, in this case apparently causing Evgeny Vladimirovich to suffocate; under conditions at the dacha an emergency tracheotomy was not possible. He died on his daughter's ninth birthday. For her recollections of his death, see Tuchin, "Suprugi Bek: Kontseptsiia 'Obshchego dela,'" in *Obshchee delo*, 8–9.—A.M.L.

14. The following account of Anna Nikolaevna's feelings after her husband's death is taken from a piece she wrote in October 1950 after finishing her memoir. Explorer and ethnographer Vladimir K. Arsenyev (1872–1930) led numerous expeditions to study the natural environment and indigenous peoples of the Russian Far East. He wrote extensively about his explorations, including the work mentioned here, *Skvoz' taigu* (Through the Taiga) (reprinted, Moscow: Mysl', 1966). The Sikhote-Alin Mountains, which run along the Sea of Japan northeast of Vladivostok, are a region of great natural beauty and biodiversity.—A.M.L.

15. By "Flamorion," Anna Nikolaevna is referring to the French astronomer Nicholas-Camille Flammarion (1842–1925), author of numerous highly popular works on astronomy for general readers, including novels such as *Stella* (1897).

16. The poem Anna Nikolaevna wrote after her husband's death appears at the end of this chapter.—A.M.L.

17. Irina K. Kakhovskaya (1888–1960) led a life far more exciting than one might expect of a kindergarten teacher. Arrested by the tsarist government in 1907 for

participation in one of the Socialist Revolutionary (SR) Party's terrorist battalions, she spent several years in forced labor in Nerchinsk before being freed in 1914 by the amnesty decreed in honor of the tercentennial of the Romanov dynasty in 1913, and settled in exile in Chita, where she and Anna Nikolaevna became acquainted. Continuing to be active in the left wing of the SR Party there, she left Chita for Petrograd when the Revolution of 1917 began, and became a prominent Left SR. Arrested in German-occupied Ukraine for plotting terrorist acts, she was condemned to death and tortured but freed when Ukraine again changed hands. During 1919 she became involved in a plot to assassinate General Anton Denikin, leader of the White Volunteer Army in southern Russia. With her history of active involvement with the Bolshevik Party's most important enemy on the Left, it is not surprising that the Soviet government arrested and imprisoned her more than once, but she survived to spend the last five years of her life in freedom, living in a provincial town in Kaluga Province south of Moscow. It is significant that Anna Nikolaevna, writing during the late Stalinist years, writes about her friend with such warmth despite her affiliation with terrorism and the Bolshevik Party's great rival, the Left SRs. See *Politicheskie deiateli Rossii 1917: Biografcheskii slovar'*, ed. P. V. Volobuev (Moscow: Bol'shaia Rossiiskaia Entsiklopediia, 1993), s.v.—A.M.L.

18. The Bolshevik Frunze (1885–1925), arrested and exiled numerous times by the tsarist government for his revolutionary activity, became one of the Red Army's most gifted commanders during the civil war. A member of the Politburo from 1924, he served as Commissar of War in 1925.—A.M.L.

19. Fistulae are hollow cavities or abscesses, in this case in bones as a result of tuberculosis.—A.M.L.

20. Located about forty miles from St. Petersburg, Schlüsselburg Prison was an ancient fortress used by the tsarist government for the incarceration of the most dangerous revolutionaries.—A.M.L.

21. If Anna Nikolaevna had joined the Bolshevik Party she would have been under pressure to renounce friendship with people belonging to other political parties.—A.M.L.

22. *Doma terpimosti*, literally, houses of tolerance, were places where registered prostitutes worked. Prostitution was legal in the Russian Empire, as long as prostitutes registered with the local police, submitted to regular medical examinations, and carried the notorious "yellow ticket."—A.M.L.

23. Literally, the Department for the Protection of Maternity and Infancy, whose main purpose was to introduce measures to reduce infant and child mortality.

24. "Workers' departments," or *rabfaki*, served as preparatory courses to enable workers and peasants to enter institutions of higher education.—A.M.L.

5. The Highs and Lows of Working Life

1. Quoted from chapter 1, "The Stages of My Life."

2. See the bibliography for major works in English on the history of Russian psychology.—A.M.L.

3. "O perekhodnom vozraste," *Prosveshchenie Sibiri*, no. 7/8 (1928).

4. In Irkutsk Anna Nikolaevna lived with her daughter in an apartment on the top floor of the "White House," formerly the governor's mansion, today the univer-

sity library. It was close to the university, and its rooms were assigned to professors. A fierce battle had taken place in and about the building between Reds and Whites during the civil war, and bullet holes and blood stains still marked the rooms and halls, according to her daughter's memoirs. It had a huge old ceramic Russian stove, but finding and carting scarce wood four flights was too difficult to do often and, more often than not, they were cold. The apartment was gay with the doings of Lyusya and her three close friends, who studied and spent their leisure time together, playing piano and singing. They and the other faculty families cooked in the former governor's kitchen where, in the evenings, the women often gathered together and sang.

5. Although I have been unable to identify this Professor Rubinshtein, he could not have been the eminent Soviet psychologist Sergei L. Rubinshtein (1889–1960), who was teaching at Novorossiisk University in Odessa at this time.—A.M.L.

6. The "myrrh-bearing women" (*zheny mironositsy*) were the women disciples of Christ, led by Mary Magdalene, who went to his tomb on the third day to anoint his body.—A.M.L.

7. "Defectology" is the term used at the time for the study and treatment of children with mental or physical handicaps.—A.M.L.

8. For Ushinsky, see chap. 3 n. 31; William James (1842–1910), was an American physician, philosopher, and psychologist, whose work on psychology combined the study of the mind with physiology and biology. Anna Nikolaevna was doubtless familiar with his major work, *The Principles of Psychology* (1890), which established psychological functionalism and the physical bases of mental processes.—A.M.L.

9. This dogmatic treatise, written by Lenin in 1908, is his major work on Marxist theory, in which he argues for strict materialist realism and refutes idealist trends in contemporary Marxist philosophy.—A.M.L.

10. "Opyt antropometricheskikh doissledovanii v ochage bolezni Beka v Zabaikal'e" (An experiment in anthropometric research in the center of Bek's Disease in Transbaikal), *Novaia khirurgiia*, no. 5 (1927).

11. French experimental psychologist Alfred Binet (1857–1911) created widely used scales for measuring intelligence in children.—A.M.L.

12. Anna Nikolaevna opposed Lyusya's marriage to Konstantin Andrusevich, although he was well known to her and was generally well liked, having lived with the Beks briefly when he was orphaned. It is not entirely clear why she was against the marriage. The official family reason was an age difference of eight years, but it is clear that there was more to it; it may be that Anna Nikolaevna thought his choice of career—animal husbandry—was insufficiently intellectual or that in some way he was Lyusya's inferior. Married to him, a state farm employee, Lyusya would not live in the university circles her mother would have chosen for her.

13. According to her daughter's memoirs, Anna Nikolaevna was not competent in any housework, and "she didn't like it." A distant relative, Sofia Ivanovna Cheremisinova, lived with her and managed the household; other relatives also occasionally lived with her for a time and helped out.

14. A training ground for future party members, the Komsomol, or Young Communist League, accepted students and young workers with politically correct class backgrounds and sought to inculcate atheism, communist political orthodoxy, and high morals into Soviet youth.—A.M.L.

15. Collective exams were introduced into Soviet schools for a brief time in the late 1920s.—A.M.L.

16. Antonina Ivanovna Serebrennikova was Anna Nikolaevna's childhood friend, Tonya Ryndina, whom she describes in her girlhood diary as in love with "the forester Serebrennikov, she finds that he has a knight's soul" (see chapter 1).

17. Situated on the Ob River, Novosibirsk was only a village when construction of the Trans-Siberian Railroad reached that point in 1893. The town that grew up as a result of the railroad was called Novonikolaevsk in honor of Tsar Nicholas II. Renamed Novosibirsk in 1925, the city grew from 107,000 inhabitants in 1917 to 404,000 in 1939, when Anna Nikolaevna lived there. A railroad hub serving the nearby Kuznetsk Basin coalfields, Novosibirsk became a major manufacturing center after factories were evacuated there from the west during World War II. Since the war it has also been the major Siberian scientific, educational, cultural, and economic center.—A.M.L.

18. Tomsk University, founded in 1888, was the first Russian university established outside European Russia.

19. In seeking to explain how neurophysical processes such as the eye's reception of light rays are transformed into meaningful mental images, Helmholtz used the metaphor of hieroglyphs to describe how external objects are turned into symbols that the brain interprets. The metaphor was adopted by the Russian psychophysiologist Sechenov and some Russian Marxists as a useful way to explain the correspondences between light reflected from external objects, neural stimuli, and visual perception, but was denounced by Lenin as an "idealist mystification." (See David Joravsky, *Russian Psychology: A Critical History* [Oxford: Basil Blackwell, 1898], 190–91.) Thus Anna Nikolaevna was denounced as being both an extreme materialist *and* an idealist at the same time.—A.M.L.

20. Konstantin N. Kornilov (1879–1957) was a leading Marxist psychologist in the 1920s, director of the Psychological Institute in Moscow from 1923, and an eclectic researcher who combined the study of physiological reactions to stimuli— he called it "reactology"—with elements of traditional subjective psychology. In the arguments over what constituted an authentic Marxist psychology at the First Congress of Pedology in January 1928, Kornilov and his followers emerged as dominant.—A.M.L.

21. It is not entirely clear what brought the local party down on Anna Nikolaevna. It could have been her continued teaching of pedology after pedology had been officially criticized. It could have been her independent attitude and her challenge to Laizan, the leader of the Marxist circle. Nor is it clear why the original negative evaluation she received from the party was replaced by a positive one. Family lore maintains that she was attacked as a pedologist and rescued by a family member in Moscow who became an academician and therefore a member of the elite. However, the man was only in his twenties at the time and not yet in any position of power. Anna Nikolaevna herself, however, felt that the incident was related to the discussions of the Marxism circle and her arguments with Laizan, and that she was rescued by a member of the party's Central Committee on the basis of the explanatory letter she had sent him.

22. On the stock farm the family was allotted rooms in an apartment in a barrack. Lyusya and Konstantin had one room, Anna Nikolaevna and the four boys, another. A third room in the apartment came to be occupied by Konstantin's sister and Anna Nikolaevna's sister-in-law Alexandra (wife of the arrested Nikolai Zhukov),

another sister, Sonya, and her child. There was a small space for a communal kitchen with a burner heated by wood. They also had steam heat provided by a furnace in the basement, the only barrack on the farm that had such a luxury. An outside toilet served the entire barrack. It was filthy and appalling in its smell. In the winter it was worse; those who recall it today say simply, "[I]t is difficult to describe its terrible condition."

APPENDIX: SUMMARY OF A LECTURE

1. For William James, see chap. 5 n. 8. Anna Nikolaevna may have been referring to Nikolai N. Lange (not Longe) (1858–1921), an early Russian psychologist interested in child development, memory, and perception, whose psychological laboratory in Odessa was one of the first such laboratories in Russia.—A.M.L.

2. For Ushinsky, see chap. 3 n. 31. Physician and anatomist Peter F. Lesgaft (1837–1909) believed in the importance of exercise for the physical and moral development of children, and founded physical education in Russia. I have not been able to identify Vodovozova.—A.M.L.

3. For Sechenov and Pavlov, see chapter 5; Wilhelm Wundt (1832–1920) was another early psychophysiologist and experimental psychologist in Germany.—A.M.L.

4. Anna Nikolaevna's frequent references to classic Russian literary works, even using fictional characters to support her arguments about human psychology, reflect the strong influence of literature on the intelligentsia of nineteenth- and early-twentieth-century Russia. For the poet Nekrasov, see chap. 1 n. 24.—A.M.L.

5. Ilya Oblomov, the protagonist of Ivan A. Goncharov's (1812–1891) best-known novel, *Oblomov* (1859), spends most of his days in bed, dreaming of the great deeds he will accomplish. His impracticality and lack of will became symbols in progressive public opinion of the superfluous and parasitic nature of the Russian nobility, as Anna Nikolaevna's allusion demonstrates.—A.M.L.

6. For Korolenko, see chap. 3 n. 14; *The History of My Contemporary* (1910–1922) is his autobiography.—A.M.L.

7. "Idiot" was the term commonly used by physicians, psychiatrists, and the general public for a mentally retarded person.—A.M.L.

8. For Séguin, see chap. 4 n. 7.

9. For Montessori, see chap. 4 n. 7.

10. Friedrich Froebel (1782–1852), a pioneering German educator and creator of the first kindergarten, became one of the most influential proponents of early childhood education in nineteenth-century Europe and the United States.—A.M.L.

11. Mikhail E. Saltykov-Shchedrin (1826–1889), civil servant, novelist, and editor of a radical journal, is best known for his devastating satires of provincial life and officialdom; the fable Anna Nikolaevna cites here uses humor and folktale motifs to condemn the economic and social inequalities of the Russian class system.—A.M.L.

12. Despite humble beginnings as the son of a peasant in the Russian far north, Mikhail V. Lomonosov (1711–1765) became Russia's most eminent scholar, scientist, poet, and linguist in the eighteenth century. Founder of the country's first university in Moscow in 1755, Lomonosov himself was called the first Russian university by poet Alexander S. Pushkin.—A.M.L.

Bibliography and Suggestions for Further Reading

MEMOIRS

The original manuscripts of Anna Nikolaevna Bek's memoir, diaries, poems, and reminiscences have been deposited in the archives of the Chita Museum, along with her daughter's unpublished memoir: Liudmila Bek-Andrusevich, "Vospominaniia o zhizni. Vstrechi s interesnymi liud'mi," and other Zhukov-Bek family papers. The published version of Anna Nikolaevna's memoir is Anna Nikolaevna Zhukova-Bek, "Obzor moei zhizni," in *Obshchee delo. Zhizn' i deiatel'nost' izvestnykh vrachei Zabaikal'ia E. V. i A. N. Bek*, comp. E. K. Andrusevich (Novosibirsk: Sibirskii khronograf, 1996).

SCHOLARLY WORKS BY A. N. BEK

"K voprosu o pedologizatsii pedogogicheskogo protsessa." *Prosveshchenie Sibiri*, no. 1 (1931): 86–93.

Kak kontrolirovat' razvitie rebenka za pervye tri goda zhizni. Irkutsk: Izdanie Irkutskogo Universiteta, 1930.

"O perekhodnom vozraste." *Prosveshchenie Sibiri*, no. 7/8 (1928): 44–53.

Osnovnye vekhi polovogo vospitaniia. Irkutsk: Izdanie Irkutskogo Universiteta, 1929.

"Protsess razvitiia myshleniia." Irkutsk: Izdanie Irkutskogo Universiteta, 1931.

Sovremennoe napravlenie v izuchenii povedeniia cheloveka (k voprosu o pskhike). Irkutsk: Izdanie Irkutskogo Universiteta, 1928.

"Urovskie bolezni (po dannym d-ra Kashina) i bolezn' Beka." *Sovetskaia meditsina*, no. 4/5 (1932).

SECONDARY SOURCES

Baraev, Vladimir. *Drevo: Dekabristy i semeistvo kandinskikh*. Moscow: Politicheskaia literatura, 1991.

Bauer, Raymond A. *The New Man in Soviet Psychology*. Cambridge, Mass.: Harvard University Press, 1959.

Bonner, Thomas Neville. *To the Ends of the Earth: Women's Search for Education in Medicine*. Cambridge, Mass.: Harvard University Press, 1992.

Engel, Barbara Alpern. *Mothers and Daughters: Women of the Intelligentsia in Nineteenth-Century Russia*. Cambridge: Cambridge University Press, 1983.

Engel, Barbara, and Clifford Rosenthal. *Five Sisters: Women against the Tsar*. Boston: Allen and Unwin, 1987.

Fitzpatrick, Sheila, ed. *Cultural Revolution in Russia, 1928–1931*. Bloomington: Indiana University Press, 1978.

Fitzpatrick, Sheila, and Yuri Slezkine, eds. *In the Shadow of Revolution: Life Stories of Russian Women.* Princeton, N.J.: Princeton University Press, 2000.

Garros, Véronique, Natalia Korenevskaya, and Thomas Lahusen. *Intimacy and Terror: Soviet Diaries of the 1930s.* New York: New Press, 1995.

Graham, Loren R. *Science, Philosophy, and Human Behavior in the Soviet Union.* New York: Columbia University Press, 1987.

Hamm, Michael F. *The City in Late Imperial Russia.* Bloomington: Indiana University Press, 1986.

Hudgins, Sharon. *The Other Side of Russia: A Slice of Life in Siberia and the Russian Far East.* College Station: Texas A&M University Press, 2003.

Isupov, V. A. "Dinamika chislennosti gorodskogo naseleniia Sibiri v periode stroitelstva sotsializma." In *Urbanizatsiia Sovetskoi Sibiri,* ed. V. V. Alekseev. Novosibirsk: Nauka, 1987.

Joravsky, David. *Russian Psychology: A Critical History.* Oxford: Basil Blackwell, 1989.

Kennan, George. *Siberia and the Exile System.* New York: Century, 1891.

Lincoln, W. Bruce. *The Conquest of a Continent: Siberia and the Russians.* New York: Random House, 1994.

Mazour, Anatole G. *The First Russian Revolution, 1825.* Stanford, Calif.: Stanford University Press, 1967.

Mehlinger, Howard, and John M. Thompson. *Count Witte and the Tsarist Government in the 1905 Revolution.* Bloomington: Indiana University Press, 1972.

Nemerov, V. *Chita: istoriia, pamiatnye mesta, sud'by.* Chita: Chitinksoe oblastnoe knizhnoe izdatel'stvo, 1994.

Petrovskii, A. V. *Psychology in the Soviet Union: A Historical Outline.* Translated by Lilia Nakhapetyan. Moscow: Progress, 1990.

Rasputin, Valentin. *Siberia, Siberia.* Translated by Margaret Winchell and Gerald Mikkelson. Evanston, Ill.: Northwestern University Press, 1996.

Stites, Richard. "Women and the Russian Intelligentsia: Three Perspectives." In *Women in Russia,* ed. Dorothy Atkinson, Alexander Dallin, and Gail Lapidus, 39–62. Stanford, Calif.: Stanford University Press, 1977.

————. *The Women's Liberation Movement in Russia: Feminism, Nihilism, and Bolshevism, 1860–1930.* Princeton, N.J.: Princeton University Press, 1978.

Tuve, Jeannette E. *The First Russian Women Physicians.* Newton, Mass.: Oriental Research Partners, 1984.

Verasaev, Vikentii Vikent'evich. *In the War: Memoirs of V. Verasaev.* Translated by Leo Wiener. New York: Mitchell Kennerley, 1917.

Wenyon, Charles. *Across Siberia on the Great Post-Road.* London: Charles H. Kelly, 1896. Reprint, New York: Arno Press and the *New York Times,* 1971.

Index

ANNE D. RASSWEILER (1933–2002) learned Russian at Smith College (B.A. 1955) and The Middlebury Summer School, and received an M.A. from Harvard University (1956) and her Ph.D. in history from Princeton University in 1980. She visited Russia for the first of many times in 1956. Accompanied by three of her four children, she spent 1975–76 at Moscow University as a Fulbright-Hays and IREX fellow. She taught Russian and Soviet history at Princeton University, Temple University, Franklin and Marshall College, and Washington College, among others. A specialist in early Soviet history, she published her first book, *The Generation of Power: The Planning and Construction of Dneprostroi, 1927–1932*, in 1988. Growing interest in Siberia led her to travel extensively there in the 1990s, and make many friends, especially in Novosibirsk. Her last trip, described in the introduction, was in 1996. She wrote numerous articles, reviews, and essays for both scholarly and general audiences on Soviet history, Siberia, and women past and present.

ADELE M. LINDENMEYR is Professor and Chair, Department of History, Villanova University, and author of *Poverty Is Not a Vice: Charity, Society, and the State in Imperial Russia*. She and Anne Rassweiler were graduate students together at Princeton.